AMAZING BIRDS

Amazing Birds

A Treasury of Facts and Trivia about the Avian World

Roger Lederer

A&CB

A & C BLACK · LONDON

CONTENTS

A QUARTO BOOK

Copyright © 2007
Quarto Publishing plc

First published in the UK
in 2007 by
A & C Black Publishers
38 Soho Square
London W1D 3HB
www.acblack.com

ISBN-13: 978-0-7136-8666-1

Conceived, designed
and produced by
Quarto Publishing plc
The Old Brewery
6 Blundell Street
London N7 9BH

QUA: BLL

Editor: *Michelle Pickering*
Designer: *Elizabeth Healey*
Picture researcher: *Claudia Tate*
Photographer: *Martin Norris*
Illustrator: *Stephen Dew*
Indexer: *Dorothy Frame*
Proofreader: *Julia Halford*
Assistant art director: *Penny Cobb*

Art director: *Moira Clinch*
Publisher: *Paul Carslake*

Colour separation by
Provision Pte Ltd, Singapore
Printed by Midas Printing
International Ltd, China

10 9 8 7 6 5 4 3 2 1

Introduction

With this richly illustrated feast of bird facts, fascinations and even a bit of folklore, you will discover a cornucopia of information about our feathered friends, much of which may surprise and even delight you. From the workings of a bird's ear to the story of the most famous carrier pigeon of WWI, you will discover fascinating insights about our closest wild companions. You will learn why birds can make nonstop migrations over long expanses of ocean, why the owl is considered wise, why some birds lay only one egg and why some birds have lost the ability to fly. Included are tips on teaching your parrot to talk, feeding birds in your garden and birdwatching. You will learn about the largest egg, heaviest bird, fastest bird and smallest bird. From silly sayings to remarkable facts and practical advice, everything you need and want to know about birds is here.

Why write such a book? Because everyone is familiar with birds, but not many of us really know birds. We recognize birds because they are the most uniform of all animal groups – all have feathers and lay eggs, many sing and most fly. It is difficult to be anywhere and not see birds around our home, office or recreation areas. Birds – colourful, tuneful and daylight-loving creatures – have been observed and studied for thousands of years. From carvings in Egyptian caves and Aristotle's writings to today's greeting cards, movies and books, bird images are everywhere. Every culture has folklore about the meaning of bird behaviour, the use of birds as medicine, stories that relate the good or bad luck a bird will bring, birds as weather forecasters and how the raven came to have a black colour. And for good reason – birds are fascinating.

Birds hear and see much better than we can, have evolved adaptations for flight, have specialized feet and beaks, migrate over long distances, make unusual sounds and are found everywhere in the world except the centre of Antarctica. But as homogeneous as they appear to be, they and their habits have diversified in amazing ways, from penguins that incubate their eggs on top of their feet to brush turkeys that do not sit on their eggs at all, and from the giant albatross of the oceans to the tiny hummingbird of the tropics. This book answers puzzles like why some birds defecate on their legs, why they fluff their feathers, why baby birds fall out of their nests, and how to attract birds to your feeder and keep them from flying into your windows.

There are many bird books published each year, but this one is unusual in its organization. It is not arranged by topic; it is not meant to be read cover to cover. Instead, it is meant to be perused a little at a time. The wide-ranging information is provided in snippets with entertaining illustrations, to be read and savoured. Open it to any page and fascinating avian facts are there to share with your friends and family. Field guides, textbooks and encyclopedias of birds are the main meal of the science of ornithology; this book is the dessert and I hope you will enjoy it.

➤ The First Bird

Although there is still discussion among avian palaeontologists, it appears that the first bird was *Archeopteryx* ('ancient wing'), which lived about 160 million years ago. It had a number of reptilian features but it also had feathers, making it a true transition form between the two groups.

160-million-year-old Archeopteryx

bird fossils as complete as this skeleton of Messelornis, a plover-like wader from 50 million years ago, are rare

NOW YOU SEE THEM, NOW YOU DON'T

✿ CHINK: Songbirds hidden in the brush announce the presence of a predator with a 'chink' call that is easily located.

✿ SEEET: When out in the open, the alarm call sounds more like 'seeet', which is a higher frequency and harder to locate.

HARRY POTTER AND HEDWIG

The Snowy Owl co-star of *Harry Potter* movie fame generated a demand for real Snowy Owls, despite it being illegal to possess them in many countries. Fortunately, the World Owl Trust successfully discouraged this mania by explaining that Snowy Owls do not make good pets.

Snowy Owls make great messengers for wizards but poor pets

ONLY THE FEATHERS

In 1894 a cat belonging to the keeper of the lighthouse on Stephens Island off the coast of New Zealand brought his master several small dead birds that turned out to be the last members of the Stephens Island Wren.

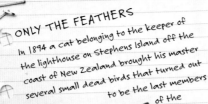

the last of the Stephens Island wrens were killed by a cat

HALF ASLEEP

Birds may sleep with one side of the brain asleep and the other awake, with sides of the brain taking turns sleeping. The eye controlled by the sleeping hemisphere is closed, while the other hemisphere's eye is open, watching for threats. This half-sleeping has only been observed in birds and aquatic mammals such as seals, whales and dolphins.

QUACK'S ECHO

A much-quoted scientific myth asserts that a duck's quack is the only sound that does not make an echo. That is problematic for two reasons:

1 Of many varieties of ducks, only a few make sounds that could be described as a quack.

2 Not making an echo in circumstances where other sounds do defies the laws of physics.

THE GREAT CREST

The Great Crested Grebe is the most well known of British grebes. Like the herons and egrets of the US in the 1800s, it was hunted for its feathers. By 1860 there were only 42 pairs in Britain. Protective laws established shortly afterwards slowly took hold and today's population is estimated at 24,000 birds.

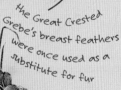

the Great Crested Grebe's breast feathers were once used as a substitute for fur

a duck's quack DOES echo!

Eurasian Jays store thousands of acorns each autumn to eat in the winter

🦅 Food Stores

✿ A Eurasian Jay may store between 6,000 and 11,000 acorns in the autumn, expecting that they will last through the next year.

✿ Scrub Jays can find their buried acorns by the orientation of the sun, even on a cloudy day.

✿ Nutcrackers bury in the soil somewhere between 70,000 and 100,000 seeds in the autumn for winter consumption. The birds have evolved a sublingual (under the tongue) pouch in which to carry as many as four dozen seeds at a time from their collection places to their caching places. Even after a snowfall the birds are able to locate 50 per cent or more of the seeds, apparently by remembering the surrounding terrain and landmarks.

HOUSE SPARROW IMMIGRANT

Several groups and individuals made efforts beginning in the 1850s to establish the House (English) Sparrow in the US. Some wanted reminders of their European homeland; others wanted to control cankerworms in Central Park, New York. By 1875 the House Sparrow had spread to San Francisco, and by 1887 some states were already establishing control programmes.

ART STUDENTS: IN EXPERIMENTS, SOME PIGEONS WERE ABLE TO TELL THE DIFFERENCE BETWEEN THE PAINTINGS OF MONET AND PICASSO. THIS DEMONSTRATES THAT PIGEONS CAN DISCRIMINATE COLOUR AND PATTERN SIMILARLY TO HUMANS.

CARRYING COALS TO NEWCASTLE

The Little Owl of southern Greece was once so common that a saying with the same meaning as 'Carrying coals to Newcastle' is 'Bringing owls to Athens' – that is, doing something unnecessary.

🦉 The Strangest Parrot

✿ The Kakapo survives in the mountains of three small islands off the coasts of New Zealand and numbers only about 50 individuals.

✿ It is the only parrot unable to fly and is also the heaviest of all parrots, weighing up to 3.5 kg (8 lb).

✿ Also known as the Owl Parrot, it is nocturnal in order to avoid predation by hawks and eagles.

✿ Feeding on leaves, buds, flowers and other vegetative material, the Kakapo leaves tracks through the vegetation as if it were a rabbit.

THE RIME OF THE ANCIENT MARINER

This poem, published in 1798, gave rise to the saying about an 'albatross around one's neck' to mean a severe burden. It apparently derived from the belief of early sailors that killing an albatross would bring bad luck to their ship. The poem was written by Samuel Taylor Coleridge, who had never seen an albatross.

illustration from an 1887 edition of
The Rime of the Ancient Mariner

Elementary, My Dear Hoatzin

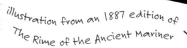

❖ The first birds of 150 million years ago had claws on their wings, but the only living bird with wing claws is the Hoatzin, a chicken-sized bird that lives in the Amazon basin of Brazil and Peru.

❖ Newly hatched birds have two claws on each wing that enable them to clamber through the vegetation before they gain the ability to fly. If they are alarmed by a predator, they dive into the water beneath the mangrove vegetation and then claw their way back onto the trees.

❖ Hoatzin are strictly vegetarians, eating the leaves, flowers and fruit of various plants. The adults ferment this food in their guts and regurgitate it to feed their young.

SEVEN HINTS FOR BIRD IDENTIFICATION

1 Find the bird with your naked eyes first; only then use binoculars, which have a magnified but restricted field of view.

2 Watch the bird for as long as you can before getting out your field guide; the guide is under your control, the bird is not.

3 Look for general impression – size, shape, behaviour, location. A small bird pecking on the side of a tree narrows down the choices considerably.

4 The silhouette is most important because colours are not always visible and can sometimes be deceiving.

5 Songs or calls, if you hear them, are bonuses if you see the bird and the only way to identify it if you cannot.

6 Buy a good field guide appropriate for the area and get some idea of what you should expect from a local bird list.

7 The best hint of all is to go birdwatching with an experienced birder.

CHOOSE A HEALTHY MATE

One of the explanations for the colourful plumage of male birds is to advertise their health to potential female mates. The colours and display signify good health, which is more important to a female bird than the showy colours themselves. A male with ragged, dull plumage might have parasites or a disease, thereby eliminating him as a suitable partner.

extravagantly plumaged male with the less showy female bird of paradise

the female Purple Martin has lighter chest plumage

LOAFING BAR

After ducks mate, the females tend to the nest and raise the young while the males move themselves to a loafing bar, where they hang out and moult their feathers into a female-like eclipse plumage. Later they moult into their next courtship plumage. Waterfowl are unusual among birds in that all the flight feathers fall out at the same time, so the males in these loafing bars are unable to fly.

a Grey Plover shaking its leg to attract food

🦅 Fancy Footwork

Most plovers and lapwing species vibrate, tap or shake their feet on the ground in order to encourage invertebrates such as worms and nematodes to come to the surface.

THE PURPLE MARTIN

✿ A large swallow, Purple Martins are purported to eat 2,000 mosquitoes a day, although the evidence for this is lacking.

✿ Once a solitary nester, building nests in cavities made by woodpeckers, Purple Martins now often nest in colonies, the holes provided for them by humans in the form of Purple Martin 'condominiums' – multi-room birdhouses available in different sizes to house different-size colonies of birds.

✿ Typical colonial nesting birds recognize their young among all the young of the colony, but Purple Martins are unable to do so. They have to learn to recognize their particular hole in the colony house.

PLOVERS' EYESIGHT

Plovers feed at night as well as during the day, necessitating some system to allow them to feed in very dim light. They can do so because they have a higher concentration of sensory cells in their retina than other wading birds. In addition, the optic lobe of plovers is almost twice that of sandpipers because plovers feed by sight, while sandpipers probe for prey with a sensitive bill tip.

FEATHER-EATING BACTERIA

Moulted feathers or feathers on a dead bird decompose rapidly due to bacteria found in soil. These bacteria are found on live birds but they cause no decay. This may be due to the fact that the preen gland contains oil with antibiotic properties, or exposure to UV radiation.

Most birds avoid chilli peppers, but not the Curve-billed Thrasher

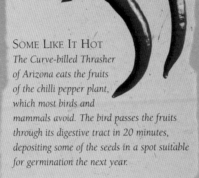

Some Like It Hot

The Curve-billed Thrasher of Arizona eats the fruits of the chilli pepper plant, which most birds and mammals avoid. The bird passes the fruits through its digestive tract in 20 minutes, depositing some of the seeds in a spot suitable for germination the next year.

DECEPTION

The White-winged Shrike-Tanager of South America acts as a guard for members of its flock and gives a warning call in case of danger. Other species have come to rely on it, but sometimes this sentinel gives a false alarm when the tanager and another bird see an insect; the false alarm distracts the other bird so the tanager can have a meal.

GROUP NAMES FOR THE JAY FAMILY

A chattering of choughs.

A murder of crows.

A party of jays.

A tiding of magpies.

A parliament of rooks.

An unkindness of ravens.

CODE NAMES

During World War II, Japanese gliders were designated with birds' names.

New World King Vulture

Do Vultures Smell?

✿ **Yes**: New World species, such as the Black, King and Turkey Vultures and the California and Andean Condors, related to storks and ibises, have the ability to smell. In fact, Turkey Vultures have been used by gas companies to detect leaks. Ethyl mercaptan, one of the gaseous components of carrion, is pumped through gas lines and wherever a crack in the line allows the escape of gas, Turkey Vultures are seen circling overhead.

✿ **No**: African and Asian vultures, related to hawks and eagles, apparently have a weak or nonexistent sense of smell.

the Bald Eagle has been the US symbol since 1782

Woodpeckers are found all over the world except for Madagascar and the Australian region.

US Symbol

✿ The Bald Eagle was chosen as the symbol for the United States in 1782, although Benjamin Franklin preferred the Wild Turkey.

✿ A Bald Eagle by the name of Old Abe was purchased from Chippewa Indians by the Eighth Wisconsin Volunteer Infantry for $5 during the American Civil War. Abe was carried into battle as a mascot, including the siege of Vicksburg in 1863. After the war, the eagle helped to raise funds for various veterans' charities.

✿ Another Bald Eagle, Challenger, was trained to fly into sports stadiums during the playing of the US national anthem, including baseball's World Series, American football's Super Bowl and basketball's NCAA Final Four. He also demonstrated his skills at the White House.

PUTTING ON THE BRAKES

Flying at 40–65 kph (25–40 mph), birds need to slow down by applying some sort of brakes. They do so in various ways.

✿ They spread their wings.

✿ They lower their tail.

✿ In the case of waterfowl and seabirds, they spread their webbed feet in front of them.

✿ Woodpeckers, landing on the side of a tree trunk, slow down their forward speed by coasting upwards and then grab the trunk when their speed is appropriate for doing so.

AUSTRALIAN APOSTLES

Living in Australia is the Apostle Bird, which lives in groups of 10–12, comprising a male, several females and immature birds. As a communal group, they build a nest and feed the nestlings. They are often seen in a group of 12, hence their name.

THE MUTE SWAN IS NOT MUTE

The Mute Swan does have a voice but, interestingly, does not use it while flying. Instead, its flight feathers make a noise that serves as communication within the flock.

The Christmas Bird Count

✿ In the late 1800s in North America, people engaged in a Christmas tradition in which hunting teams were formed to see who could bring in the most birds and mammals. Because of traditions like this and other pressures on wild bird populations, American ornithologist Frank Chapman of the then newly formed Audubon Society, which focuses on the conservation of birds and their habitats, proposed a different holiday tradition: counting birds instead of shooting them.

✿ The first Christmas Bird Count in 1900 saw 27 counters tally a total of 90 species of birds. The bird counts have continued for over a century, producing the largest database in ornithology.

✿ The activity has now spread over North and South America, with more than 50,000 observers participating in the all-day census of winter bird populations.

the Bell-Boeing Osprey

AIRPLANES WITH BIRD NAMES

Bell-Boeing Osprey
Gloster Gannet
Fairey Fulmar and Gannet
Schweizer Condor
Lockheed Hummingbird

list continues on page 18

get some binoculars and start counting birds

The Big Garden Birdwatch

According to the Royal Society for the Protection of Birds, a record 470,000 people, including 86,000 children, participated in a recent survey of British birds. The most common bird of the 80 species and 8 million birds seen was the House Sparrow. Since 1999, the UK government has considered the populations of wild birds to be an indicator of the quality of life in the UK.

THE BREEDING BIRD SURVEY

In North America, this survey is a cooperative effort between the US Geological Survey's Patuxent Wildlife Research Center and the Canadian Wildlife Service's National Wildlife Research Centre to monitor the status and trends of North American bird populations. Birds are surveyed and data collected by thousands of knowledgeable volunteers to compile population data on more than 400 bird species. A similar survey for the UK is organised by the British Trust for Ornithology.

a Blue-footed Booby reveals its age in its feet

🦉 How Old?

It is difficult to assess the age of a bird, but there are a couple of methods.

Method 1: A rough indication of a young bird's age can be had by blowing apart the feathers on the skull and looking for dark areas. These are areas where the skull has not yet formed (like a baby's head). The age of a bird in months up to about a year of age can be told, but this technique is not reliable for older birds.

Method 2: A new technique has been developed that tests the level of the chemical pentosidine in the bird's skin or foot webbing. This chemical accumulates in a bird's tissues as it ages.

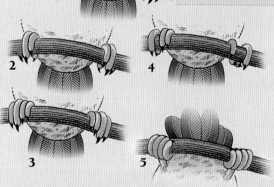

Bar-tailed Godwit, aka Limosa lapponica

SCIENTIFIC NAMES EXPLAINED

❖ The scientific name of a bird has two parts: the genus and the species.

❖ The genus is always capitalized, while the species name is not.

❖ Both are written in italics or underlined – for example, the Canada Goose is *Branta canadensis* and the Common Swift is *Apus apus*.

❖ Both the singular and plural form of the word species is species; the word specie means a gold coin.

❖ Although sometimes referred to as Latin names, scientific names are also derived from Greek, Russian, Old English and other languages.

airplanes with bird names – list continued from page 17

list continued from page 17

Hawker-Siddeley Kestrel
McDonnell Douglas/British Aerospace Harrier
DeHaviland Albatross
Curtis Eagle
Sikorsky Eagle
Howard Nightingale
LWF Owl
Kellett Hughes Flying Crane
Cessna Skyhawk
Grumman Albatross, Duck, Goose, and Wigeon
Curtis Wright Kingbird
Curtis Falcon, Helldiver, Raven, and Seahawk
Bell Helo Blackbird
Lockheed Blackbird
Ryan Seagull
Northrop Bantam
Beech Jayhawk
GM Turkey

STRONG TOES

Mousebirds of southern Africa have a special toe structure, allowing them to do the following:

1 They can have three toes forward and one back.
2 Two toes forward and two back.
3 All toes forward.
4 The toe position of each foot may be different simultaneously.
5 They can hang upside down from a branch to feed or sleep.

The Barnacle Goose

is that a goose or a barnacle?

A goose of the far north, the Barnacle Goose was so named because early observers thought the young geese hatched out of barnacles. Barnacles, attached to rocks in the tidal zone, filter feed with feather-like appendages waving in the water, apparently reminding someone of young birds hatching from an egg.

DOUBLE DUTY

Heliconia plants of some islands of the Caribbean grow in two forms: one red and one green or greenish yellow. They are also different shapes to fit the bills of the Purple-throated Carib Hummingbirds.

❖ The male's beak fits the shorter red flowers.
❖ The female's beak, 30 per cent longer, fits the green flowers. This assures the pollination of the plant species.

UPS AND DOWNS

There are two major groups of ducks: dabblers and divers.

✿ Dabblers float on the surface of the water and tip up their rear ends so that their bills dip into the water to feed on shallow plants and animals.
✿ Divers do just that, dive below the surface, in deeper water.

DDT

DDT, a pesticide banned in developed countries but still used in nations where malaria continues to be a major health problem, accumulates in the food chain and is toxic to many birds. Effects include brain shrinkage, eggshell thinning and interference with nerve transmission. Bald Eagles, Peregrine Falcons and Brown Pelicans were the best known of birds whose populations declined due to DDT. As a result of eggshell thinning, the parent birds would actually crush their eggs when incubating them.

Brown Pelican from John James Audubon's Birds of America

🦩 Aptosochromatism

Until about 1900 it was believed that birds only moulted once a year and that the change in plumage colour was due to the ability of feathers to change colour, a phenomenon called aptosochromatism. However, feathers are dead structures once they are fully formed and cannot change colour. It is moulting – the loss of old feathers and the growth of new ones – that produces different-coloured feathers. Some species also change plumages by feather wear. As the feathers get shorter, the colours underneath those feathers show. For example, European Starlings change from a glossy black to a white spotted plumage as the black feathers shorten and the spots on the feathers underneath appear.

feathers do not have the ability to change colour (aptosochromatism)

RAREST SPECIES

It is hard to say exactly which species are the rarest because rare birds are so hard to find and count.

- **Spix's Macaw** of Brazil – the last known bird living in the wild disappeared in 2000; possibly extinct, it is likely that any remaining population is tiny (a small number survive in captivity).
- **Magdalena** and **Kalinowski's Tinamous** of South America – no recent sightings.
- **Hooded Seedeater** of Brazil – fewer than 50 birds survive.
- **Amsterdam Albatross** of the far southern Indian Ocean – about 90 birds.
- **Pink-headed Duck** of India and Nepal – last seen in 1949.
- **Cuban Kite** of Cuba – extremely small population.
- **California Condor** of California – 50 in the wild, 97 in captivity.

list continues on page 22

SMALLEST AND LARGEST OWLS

- ❀ The smallest owl in the world is the sparrow-sized Elf Owl of the southwestern United States, at a length of 13–14 cm ($5^1/_8$–$5^1/_2$ in). It weighs only 40 g (1.4 oz).

- ❀ The Eurasian Eagle Owl is the largest owl, at a length of 58–71 cm (23–28 in). It can weigh up to 4 kg (140 oz).

BUG BEDFELLOWS

- ❀ Ten per cent of all parrot species choose active termite mounds as the location for their nest. Although annoyed at first, the termites eventually adjust and seal off the parrot nest from the rest of the termite mound.

- ❀ The Yellow-rumped Cacique, a member of the blackbird family, nests in the upper Amazon basin. It has a hanging sac-like nest and nests in colonies in trees with wasp nests. Studies have shown that the advantage of nesting near the wasps is that the wasps keep botflies away; otherwise, the botflies would lay eggs on the young birds and the botfly larvae would feed on them.
- ❀ The Dark Chanting Goshawk of Africa camouflages its nest with the webs of social spiders.

the Yellow-rumped Cacique nests near wasps

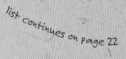

a thankful Chimney Swift

IN THANKS

It was once thought that the Chimney Swift, which nests in chimneys, dropped a young swift down the chimney in a gesture of thanks before finally leaving the homesite.

RELATIVE EGG SIZE

Although large birds lay larger eggs than small birds, small birds have proportionately larger eggs and clutches relative to their body size.

❀ Sixty ostrich eggs equal the weight of one adult ostrich, but it takes only about nine hummingbird eggs to weigh as much as the hummingbird.

❀ About the size of a chicken, kiwis lay the largest eggs proportionate to the bird's body size; it takes only four kiwi eggs to equal the weight of an adult kiwi.

❀ The Mute Swan lays an egg that is 4 per cent of its body weight and its entire clutch comprises 23 per cent of its body weight. Compare that to the Blue Tit, $1/900$th the weight of the swan. The tit lays an egg about 12 per cent of its body weight and a clutch that comprises 130 per cent of its body weight.

CORN CRAKE CALL

The call of the Corn Crake, a relative of the rails, can be imitated by brushing a credit card over the teeth of a comb.

sixty ostrich eggs equal the weight of an adult ostrich

WOODCOCK PIN-FEATHERS

The small feather at the base of the first primary feather of each wing is known as the pin-feather in the US and as the alula or bastard wing in the UK (where the term pin-feather usually refers to a new, growing feather or a narrow tail feather). The pin-feather of the American Woodcock and some Asian snipe was a valued tool of many artists for 'pin-feather painting'.

❖ It was a prized possession of watercolour painters.

❖ It was used to draw the gold stripe down the side of the Rolls-Royce.

❖ The pin-feather was also used for putting stripes on bicycle frames.

❖ Artists used it to paint cameos on ivory.

❖ It was used for adding the painted detail on toy soldiers.

pin-feathers were used to paint stripes on bicycles

BEST SNIFFERS

1 The Snowy Petrel has the largest olfactory bulb (where the olfactory nerves terminate) in relation to the size of the forebrain. This bird feeds on the odiferous carcasses of seals, whales and other carrion in the Antarctic.

2 The second largest olfactory bulb to forebrain ratio belongs to kiwis, which feed mainly on earthworms.

the kiwi has nostrils at the end of its bill and an acute sense of smell

rarest species –
list continued from page 20

- ❖ **Grenada Dove** of Grenada – perhaps 100 individuals.
- ❖ **Thick-billed Ground Dove** of the Solomon Islands – fewer than 50 survive.
- ❖ **Kakapo** (Owl Parrot) of Australia – fewer than 50 survive.
- ❖ **Sulu Hornbill** of the Philippines – fewer than 40.
- ❖ **Tahiti Monarch** of French Polynesia – only 18 individuals survive.
- ❖ **Pale-headed Brush Finch** of Ecuador – 10 to 32 remain.
- ❖ **Bachman's Warbler** of the US – last seen in 1988.
- ❖ **Bali Myna** of Bali, Indonesia – none left in the wild, but many in captivity.
- ❖ **Hawaiian Crow** of Hawaii – only three remain.

UNSUBSTANTIATED WEATHER FORECASTS

- ❖ Birds fly low when bad weather is coming.
- ❖ Birds do not fly at all in bad weather.
- ❖ Birds make more sounds than they usually do when a low-pressure centre approaches.

ENOUGH SAID: THE RUFF HAS THE LARGEST TESTES OF ALL SANDPIPERS. IN BREEDING SEASON, NEARLY 5 PER CENT OF ITS BODY WEIGHT IS TESTES – EVEN MORE THAN ITS BRAIN.

many composers have been inspired by birds and birdsong

SUN PROTECTION

Many insectivorous birds have dark-coloured feathers in front of their eyes, which might serve to reduce glare and make capturing insects easier.

LISTS, LISTS, LISTS

One of the appeals of birdwatching is making a list of birds seen. The most common is the life list – the number of different bird species seen in one's life. However, there are many others – daily lists; yearly lists; province, county, city and shire lists. Also TV lists, zoo lists, movie lists and so on. This listing apparently satisfies the need to collect without harming anything.

Musical Inspiration

✿ 'Sumer is icumen in' is a thirteenth-century piece of music from Britain in which the cuckoo is imitated as 'Cuccu cuccu, wel singes thu cuccu'.

✿ Vivaldi named a flute concerto *Il Gardellino* (The Goldfinch), having been inspired by the bird.

✿ *The Ballet of the Unhatched Chickens* by Russian composer Musorgsky describes the hatching of chickens.

Backpacking

Western Grebes

Grebes have two or three young that hatch in a floating nest. If the hatchlings get cold, they call to their parents to incubate them. When all are hatched, the young abandon the nest and clamber upon the back of an adult, where they are ferried around. When the mate arrives with food, the carrier shakes the chicks off and feeds them as they swim. The adult grebes will dive to escape danger even if they have chicks on their back.

hey, I'm not lazy, but who's going to say no to a free ride?

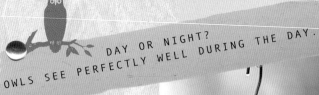

DAY OR NIGHT? OWLS SEE PERFECTLY WELL DURING THE DAY.

BIRDS NAMED AFTER PEOPLE (MAINLY NORTH AMERICAN)

ABERT'S Towhee

VAUX'S Swift

McKAY'S Bunting

BRANDT'S Cormorant

STELLER'S Eider and Jay

CASSIN'S Finch and Kingbird

CLARK'S Nutcracker and Grebe

BAIRD'S Sandpiper and Sparrow

HUTTON'S Vireo

BELL'S Vireo

HAMMOND'S Flycatcher

ROSS'S Gull and Goose

THAYER'S Gull

SWAINSON'S Hawk

COSTA'S Hummingbird

NUTTALL'S Woodpecker

LEWIS'S Woodpecker

FRANKLIN'S Gull

AUDUBON Shearwater

WILLIAMSON'S Sapsucker

NELSON'S Sharp-tailed Sparrow

list continues on page 26

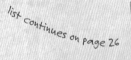

FEEDER CAUTIONS

To reduce fatal collisions with window glass from birds approaching feeders:

1 Angle the glass 20–40 degrees downwards.

2 Use tinted glass.

3 Put a screen or net in front of the glass.

4 Place opaque objects 5–10 cm (2–4 in) in front of the glass.

5 Place bird feeders less than 2 m (2 yds) or more than 10 m (10 yds) in front of the glass.

6 Spray the glass with vegetable oil or artificial snow to make it visible.

don't put feeders near windows

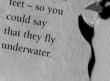

FLYING PENGUINS

Penguins swim with their wings, not their webbed feet – so you could say that they fly underwater.

an owl's facial structure affects its hearing

Face of an Owl

❁ The circle of feathers around an owl's eyes, called a facial disc, is the bird's most characteristic feature.

❁ The flatness of the disc and the structure of the feathers serve to enhance the hearing of nocturnal owls by funnelling sound to the ears. The ears are also asymmetrical in shape and position to help determine the location of sounds.

❁ Diurnal and crepuscular owls (those active during daylight and twilight) do not have as well developed a facial disc because they do not rely on their hearing to source prey as much as nocturnal owls do.

seed-eating House Finches

flock of Snow Geese

COUNTING BIRDS

Studies have demonstrated that observers estimating large numbers of birds in flocks by eye underestimate by an average of 50 per cent.

SEED EATING

Finches and sparrows do not simply bite a seed to open it. Instead, the lower mandible moves back and forth until the seed opens. When it is partially open, the mandible moves side to side to remove the rest of the husk.

ALARM CALLS

Many birds signal their mates or others in their flock with predator alarm calls that vary in intensity, frequency and quality, imparting such information as distance and dangerousness of the predator. For example, swallows have a particular alarm call when they see a Hobby (this bird of prey often attacks and eats swallows). There may also be differences in alarm calls in response to terrestrial versus non-terrestrial predators.

The Pink Flamingo

✿ Flamingos get their bright pink coloration from pigments called carotenoids, found in their diet of invertebrates such as small shrimp, algae and diatoms.

✿ In zoos, their diet may be supplemented with carrot derivatives to maintain this colour. Otherwise, they would be white.

✿ In legend, flamingos are the birds that rose from the ashes – the mythical firebird known as the phoenix – thus getting reddish pink on their wings.

✿ In 1946, the American company Union Products started manufacturing 'Plastics for the Lawn'. Their collection included dogs, ducks, frogs and pink flamingos. As Americans moved to the suburbs with their large lawns, ornaments such as the flamingo became increasingly popular. By the 1970s the plastic pink flamingo had become the symbol of bad taste and anti-environmentalism, although some people still enjoy annoying their neighbours with these artificial birds.

Pink flamingos were used as croquet mallets in Lewis Carroll's surreal Alice in Wonderland

seagulls – worldwide birds

Pirates

A number of carnivorous birds, rather than seeking and capturing their own prey, engage in piracy by stealing the prey of other species. It is a profitable tactic. In a study of the Aplomado Falcon of Mexico, piracy attempts were successful 82 per cent of the time, while individual hunting was successful only 38 per cent of the time.

GULLS ARE UBIQUITOUS

Gulls are found all over the world and breed on every continent, including the Arctic, the Antarctic and up to a height of 5,000 m (16,400 ft) in the Andes.

birds named after people (mainly North American) – *list continued from page 24*

LINCOLN'S Sparrow

LECONTE'S Sparrow

BOTTERI'S Sparrow

KITTLITZ'S Murrelet

XANTU'S Murrelet

COOK'S Petrel

LEACH'S Storm Petrel

WILSON'S Warbler, Phalarope, Plover and Storm Petrel

BEWICK'S Wren

HARRIS'S Sparrow

HENSLOW'S Sparrow

BONAPARTE'S Gull

an eagle's exceptional sight helps it to track fast prey

Making Accommodation

As a bird moves, or objects move in front of it, the bird's eyes have to adjust to the changing distance. Done automatically by a process called accommodation, small muscles pull the eye lens to change its focusing distance. In predatory birds such as hawks and owls, accommodation ability is exceptional in order to follow fast-moving prey.

I'm hatching an escape plan

CRACKING EGGS

An egg tooth is a small bump on the beak of birds and reptiles that helps the egg-encased young to crack the eggshell and initiate hatching. They also have a hatching muscle on the back of the neck to provide the strength to crack the egg. Both the egg tooth and muscle atrophy after hatching.

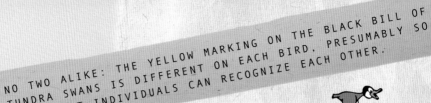

chocolate eggs are too tempting for most people to resist

FIND AN EGG?

The best thing to do with an egg that you find not in a nest is simply to leave it alone. This might be an egg that was taken and dropped by a predator or removed from the nest when the parents determined it was an unviable egg. Whatever the reason, it is likely that the egg is not going to hatch because it was most likely damaged when moved.

Duck Hunting History

In the early years of the twentieth century, waterfowl were slaughtered in great numbers in marsh areas. There were guns so large that they had to be mounted on a boat; these guns could kill dozens of birds with one blast. Fully automatic shotguns also became popular at that time. Duck populations were hard hit. Nowadays, there are many sanctuary areas for wildfowl, and a limited shooting season. In addition, many waterfowl hunters belong to organizations that advocate habitat protection for waterfowl.

SMALL TO LARGE

The smallest bird in the world is the Bee Hummingbird of Cuba. It would take 100,000 Bee Hummingbirds to tip the scales at the same weight as the biggest bird, the ostrich.

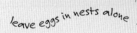

leave eggs in nests alone

First Bird Book

The first text on ornithology, *De Arte Venandi cum Avibus* (*The Art of Falconry*), was completed in 1248 by the Germanic king Frederick II von Hohenstaufen.

approximately 1,000 bird-related books are now published each year

a canary being used to detect gas in a coal mine in the 1920s

The Canary in the Mine

Caged canaries were used in coal mines from early in the twentieth century as detectors of carbon monoxide gas, to which they are particularly sensitive. A sickened or dead canary meant trouble. Today, sophisticated equipment has replaced the canary, but the phrase 'canary in the mine' persists to indicate a warning sign.

the Crow & Gate, one of 3,000 UK pubs named after birds

BIRDS NAMED AFTER PEOPLE (MAINLY EUROPEAN)

SAVI's Warbler

CETTIS's Warbler

CRETZSCHMAR's Bunting

BAILLON's Crake

PALLAS's Reed Bunting, Gull, Fish Eagle, Warbler and Grasshopper Warbler

ELEONORA's Falcon

VERREAUX's Eagle

SABINE's Gull

MONTAGU's Harrier

DUPONT's Lark

TEMMINCK's Lark and Stint

KRÜPER's Nuthatch

TENGMALM's Owl

BULWER's Petrel

FEA's Petrel

ZINO's Petrel

BOLLE's Pigeon

BERTHELOT's Pipit

BLYTH's Pipit and Reed Warbler

KITTLITZ's Plover

LICHTENSTEIN's Sandgrouse

GÜLDENSTÄDT's Redstart

EVERSMANN's Redstart

WHITE's Thrush

SWINHOE's Storm Petrel

BEWICK's Swan

RÜPPELL's Warbler

BONELLI's Warbler

MARMORA's Warbler

PUBLIC HOUSE NAMES

At least 3,000 public house names in the UK are bird related, including:

Bustard

Cock and Pheasant

Old Crow

Duck Pond

Magpie and Crown

Sociable Plover

Three Swallows

Dog and Partridge

Charrington

Crow & Gate

NUMBERS OF BIRDS

Scientists estimate that there are between 100 and 200 billion adult birds alive on the planet at any one time.

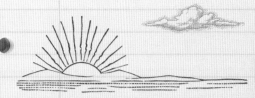

🦉 Can Birds Predict the Weather?

It is commonly believed that birds perch more before a storm. This has some basis in fact because it requires more energy to fly in low-pressure air, indicating bad weather, than in high-pressure air, so birds are more likely to perch. However, the old English countryside custom of hanging dead kingfishers by a thread to see which way they would swing and predict the wind is not as scientifically based.

GOATSUCKERS

An interesting group of birds is that called nightjars or goatsuckers. This group includes birds such as the European, Red-necked and Egyptian Nightjars as well as the Whip-poor-will. Nightjars or goatsuckers were once thought by European farmers to latch onto a goat's teat and suck out all its milk during the night. Their habit of flying at dusk and just before daylight added to their mysterious reputation.

RED IS BEST

❖ Northern Cardinal males are red but the intensity varies. Redder males tend to obtain and hold better territories, attract more fertile females and thus have more young each year.

❖ The Red-winged Blackbird has red shoulders. The males raise these colourful feathers and make their distinctive call (*oh-gurggle-eee*) in order to establish territories and defend these against other males. An experiment in which the red shoulders were painted black clearly demonstrated the importance of the red shoulders – the males with painted shoulders (no red) were unable to defend their territories.

❖ Of the flowers that birds pollinate, over 80 per cent are red or orange. Although insects such as bees can see red flowers, they cannot see red as well as birds. Hence, nectar-feeding birds prefer red flowers and bees prefer blue ones.

❖ The Royal Flycatcher of Central America has a large red fan-like crest on its head that it can erect and turn sideways. Accompanied by an open mouth, the feather display appears to be an antipredator behaviour.

bright red Northern Cardinal males are more successful than paler ones

during bad weather, birds are disoriented by the lights on telecommunications towers; many fly into the towers and die

HONEY-TONGUED HUMMINGBIRDS

The hummingbird tongue is supported by a long hyoid bone, like that in the woodpecker, that wraps around the skull and allows a long extension of the tongue out of the beak. The end of the tongue is fringed, not unlike a mop. When the hummingbird sticks its tongue into the nectar of a flower, the nectar is sopped up by these fringes by capillary action. When the tongue is pulled back into the beak, the nectar is wrung out.

Kansas Fog Disaster

At least 5,000 and maybe up to 10,000 birds died in western Kansas on the night of 22 January 1998. There was dense fog that night and the aviation safety lights on a 128 m (420 ft) radio tower reflected off this fog and disoriented the migrating birds. Flocks circled the lighted tower repeatedly and many collided with the tower and its supporting cables. Some birds hit the ground with full force and were impaled by wheat stubble, indicating that they were so disoriented that they could not tell which way was up and flew full speed into the ground.

BALD BIRDS

It is not uncommon to see a bald bird; feathers are lost off the head due to feather parasites, malnutrition or disease. This is almost always a temporary condition.

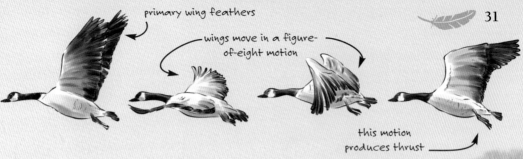

primary wing feathers

wings move in a figure-of-eight motion

this motion produces thrust

How Do Birds Fly?

❖ The outer wing feathers, called primaries, are moved forward and back in a figure-of-eight pattern, acting as a propeller to produce thrust.

❖ The inner feathers of the wing, the secondaries, produce lift as the bird's body is pulled through the air.

❖ Birds with smaller and shorter wings flap faster because they depend on more speed to keep them aloft. Birds with larger wings are able to flap more slowly because the wings provide more lift.

❖ In general, bigger birds fly faster than smaller birds because the increased weight requires a faster speed to generate lift.

ELEVEN GOOD BIRDHOUSE FEATURES

1 A roof to protect against rain and provide shade.

2 Seams of house sealed with waterproof caulk.

3 No perches – they enable predators to harass the birds.

4 Right-size entrance hole with smooth edges.

5 Ventilation to prevent overheating.

6 Drainage holes in floor.

7 Deep enough to deter predators, but shallow enough so nestlings can exit.

8 Side with hole is rough on the inside so nestlings can climb out.

9 A side, back or top that opens for inspection and cleaning after the breeding season.

10 Can be securely mounted on a pole, fence or tree.

11 Made of untreated wood or similar nontoxic material; never metal.

MADE IN CHINA

Mandarin Ducks are nearly as common in the UK than in their native lands in Asia. They have been in Britain for 75 years, but it was not until 1971 that they were accepted as British birds.

Mandarin Ducks are symbols of marital happiness in China

A good birdhouse will attract birds and keep them safe

Australian Magpies defend
their nests vigorously

TYPES OF
BIRD FEEDERS

MAGPIE WARS
Every year in Australia, magpies defending their nests attack and sometimes injure hundreds of people who stroll under the nesting trees. Australian wildlife officials recommend placing large artificial eyes on headgear or wearing protective hats or helmets.

1 Hummingbird feeders hold liquid, are made of glass or plastic and have very narrow openings or a small tube.

2 Bowl feeders are simply hanging bowls, usually covered by a large plastic dome.

3 Hopper feeders are the typical bird feeders and come in many sizes and shapes. These hold seeds that spill out of the bottom as the birds eat.

4 Suet feeders are wire or mesh baskets or large pinecones that hold suet – fat or peanut butter – with or without embedded seeds.

5 Platform feeders are simply flat surfaces mounted on a pole, stump, in a tree or extending from an outdoor windowsill.

6 Tube feeders are tall cylindrical tubes with openings and perches along the tube.

Largest Tongue
The specialized bills of the flamingo are bent in the middle with fine hair-like extensions along their edges. The top bill fits into the lower bill and the bird feeds with its head upside down in the water. The thick muscular tongue, largest in the bird world, pumps water in and out of the bill, filtering out the microorganisms that are the flamingo's diet.

flamingos have the largest and fleshiest tongues in the bird world

hopper feeders are available in many shapes and sizes

vintage South American travel poster featuring a toucan

a dark-green emu egg

THE HANDY EMU

✿ Colonial settlers of Australia ate emu meat.

✿ They used emu oil to fuel their lanterns.

✿ An emu's egg could feed a family of four for breakfast.

RIO

BRANIFF *International* AIRWAYS

WHIFFLING

When ducks and geese come in for a landing, they tip from side to side, spilling air from their wings, and often turning upside down for a brief moment in order to lose altitude. This is called whiffling. When close to the ground, they spread their wings and tail to slow their speed for landing.

TOUCAN MARKETEER

The distinctive toucan, with its large brightly coloured bill, is an extremely popular symbol used by a wide variety of businesses for mascots and names.

✿ The Toucan was the symbol for Guinness Beer until 1982.

✿ The cartoon character Toucan Sam is the mascot for the Froot Loops cereal brand.

✿ The Toucans are a Seattle-based steel drum band.

✿ Toucan Market is a purveyor of health products.

✿ The Toucan Trail is a hotel tourism marketing effort in Belize.

✿ Toucan Technologies makes cabinets for scientific laboratories.

✿ There is a telecommunications company called Toucan.

✿ Toucan is the name of a venture capital fund.

✿ A brand of car silencers is named after the bird.

✿ There is a Toucan website design business.

✿ Toucan is the name of a health market communications company.

✿ It is also the name of a company producing computerized 3D models of fish, flowers and insects.

✿ There is an ocean diving centre called Toucan.

✿ Toucan is the name of a car headlights and brakes brand.

✿ There is a business card production company of that name.

✿ A promotional golf club company is called Toucan.

Canadian stamp featuring Canada Geese

ANTING

❖ Many songbird species pick up single ants or small groups and rub them on their feathers. Other songbirds perform this act of 'anting' by spreading their wings and lying on an anthill, allowing ants to swarm up among their feathers.

❖ The reason for anting seems to be that the secretions of ants provide some protection against parasites, fungi and bacteria that may reside in birds' feathers.

❖ Birds have been seen anting with objects that are not ants, such as mothballs, apple peels and even cigarette butts.

DUETS

More than 200 species of birds are known to sing duets. They do not sing at the same time, but the male and female answer each other very quickly, so that it sounds like one bird. They may practise for months before the duet is smooth. On rare occasions a third bird off in the distance may join in to make it a trio.

DIVING FOR PREY

Falcons do not dive directly onto their prey, even though that might be the fastest route to their target. Falcons cannot see clearly directly in front of them, but if they turned their head while diving they would induce aerodynamic drag. They therefore pursue their prey in a spiral pattern – a bit slower, but with a clearer field of vision.

male Guianan
Cock-of-the-Rock

COCK-OF-THE-ROCK

These spectacular orange-and-black birds of South America get their name from their habit of nesting on cliff rock faces or large boulders. They are also fruit eaters and plant dispersers, swallowing seeds whole and defecating them elsewhere.

BIRD-RELATED TOWNS

Dunnockshaw, Lancashire, England

Kite's Hardwick, Warwickshire, England

Eaglesfield, Dumfries and Galloway, Scotland

Swansea, West Glamorgan, Wales

Bird-in-Hand, Pennsylvania, US

Wren, Oregon, US

Chicken, Alaska, US

Birdseye, Indiana, US

Goose Pimple Junction, Virginia, US

Parrot, Kentucky, US

Turkey, Texas, US

Turkey Scratch, Arkansas, US

Kingfisher, Oklahoma, US

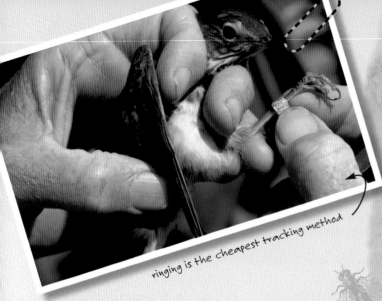

ringing is the cheapest tracking method

✈ Tracking Birds

There are several methods of tracking birds to study their migration.

✿ Ringing or banding involves attaching a ring or band to the leg of a bird to identify it. It is inexpensive and can be put on any size bird. Although not a lot of ringed birds are recovered later, the information gleaned is invaluable. Of all the birds that are ringed, only about 1 per cent of songbirds and 10 per cent of waterfowl are reported again.

✿ Small radios, as little as 1 g (1/32 oz) in weight, can be placed on birds. Although the transmitters and receivers are expensive, they are relatively accurate, and the bird can be tracked by aircraft within a 30 km (18 mile) radius or from the ground within a 10 km (6 mile) radius.

✿ Satellite telemetry can be used as well. It is very accurate and data can be gathered instantaneously, but it is also very expensive and the smallest transmitter weighs 20 g (3/4 oz), so it can only be used on larger birds.

BIRD NICKNAMES

Alba Wag	Pied or White Wagtail
Barwit	Bar-tailed Godwit
Bonxie/Bongo	Great Skua
Burger	Black-headed Gull
Bustard	Any uncooperative bird; one that is hard to get out of the brush
Buteo	Any soaring buzzard
Camp Robber	Gray Jay
Capper	Capercaillie
Casp	Caspian Tern
Willow Chiff	Chiffchaff or Willow Warbler
Commic	Common or Arctic Tern
Fly	Flycatcher
Glauc	Glaucous Gull
Glodfinch	Goldfinch
Greatspot	Great Spotted Woodpecker
Green Wood	Green Woodpecker
Gropper	Grasshopper Warbler
Hummer	Hummingbird
Kitt	Kittwake
Lapp	Lapland Bunting
Med Gull	Mediterranean Gull
LBJ	Little Brown Job – any small, nondescript bird
Leo	Long-eared Owl
Linnet	House Finch

list continues on page 38

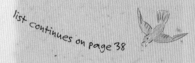

BODY TEMPERATURES

Birds' body temperatures fall in the range of 37.7–43.5°C (99.8–110.3°F), somewhat higher than mammals' at 36–39°C (96.8–102.2°F) and humans' at 37°C (98.6°F).

BANGLADESHI WATERCOCK

In Bangladesh, people collect the eggs of the Watercock and put them in a half coconut shell. They tie this against their body and carry it with them until the eggs hatch three weeks later. The birds are prized for food and fighting.

many birds eat mistletoe

MISTLETOE USES BIRDS

Mistletoe grows as a parasite on trees. It finds its way into a tree through the droppings of birds that ate mistletoe berries and excreted the seeds or wiped the sticky seeds off their bill. Various species of mistletoe are found across the world and many species of birds eat the berries; in Australia, there is the very attractive Mistletoe Bird.

BIRD GLUE

✿ The Crested Treeswift of southeast Asia constructs a small nest of feathers on a limb high up in a tree. A single egg is glued, with saliva, to the nest.

✿ The Palm Swifts of Asia and Africa construct a nest of feathers on the underside of oil palm leaves, using their sticky saliva to hold it together. At the bottom of the nest is a small ledge on which the female lays two eggs, gluing them to the nest with more saliva.

✿ The Edible-nest Swiftlets of southeast Asia construct their nests almost entirely out of saliva.

GREAT SKUA FERTILIZER

Great Skuas, predatory birds related to gulls, are sometimes blamed for attacking sheep and killing an occasional lamb. Although the birds do seem to congregate around flocks of sheep, it may actually be the other way around. Non-breeding skuas tend to congregate on grasslands, leaving their guano (droppings) to fertilize the grass, to which the sheep are naturally attracted.

➤ Mate or Be Eaten

Several studies of songbirds indicate that the males that are most brightly coloured, that most actively display, have the most obvious perches and/or have the most attractive song are most likely to attract females. However, these males are also most likely to be eaten by predators. Being obvious obviously has advantages and disadvantages.

The brightly coloured Lilac-breasted Roller attracts females with its dramatic courtship flight

a European Sparrowhawk killed by striking window glass

Window Woes

❀ Glass windows kill more birds in the US each year than any other human factor – between 100 million and 1 billion.

❀ The death toll worldwide of birds killed by striking window glass is in the billions.

❀ One and a half per cent of the entire population of Swift Parrots in Tasmania is killed annually by colliding with window glass.

bird nicknames – list continued from page 36

LRP	Little Ringed Plover
Merg	Red-breasted Merganser
Mippit	Meadow Pipit
Oik	Oystercatcher
Pec Sand	Pectoral Sandpiper
Pecker	Woodpecker
Peep	Small wading bird
Pullover	Any plover
Ravenous	Raven
Ringo	Ringed Plover
Rouzel	Ringed Ouzel
Sand	Sandpiper
Screwer	Any skua
Speck	White-fronted Goose
Sprig	Northern Pintail
Snow Bird	Junco
Turt	Turtle Dove
TV	Turkey Vulture
Tystie	Black Guillemot
Wag	Any wagtail
Woodie	Wood Pigeon

WHAT DO YOU CALL A FLOCK OF VULTURES?

The flock is called a venue. Circling vultures rising and falling on warm air currents are called a kettle, after the water bubbles in boiling water.

GOURMET DELICACIES

❖ In eighteenth-century England, birds such as the wheatear were trapped in horsehair nooses placed around their nesting sites. They were quite a delicacy at that time.

❖ In ancient Rome, flamingo tongues were considered a great delicacy.

❖ In northern Italy, France and Cyprus, migratory songbirds were eaten as gourmet delicacies. Although now illegal, high prices are still paid to sample such dishes.

LONGEST-DISTANCE MIGRATION

❀ Arctic Terns migrate the farthest of any animal, travelling from the far northern polar regions down to Antarctica. They breed in the Arctic above the 50th parallel and as the summer wanes, about three months after they first arrived in the Arctic, they begin to head south.

❀ Their four-month journey takes them 17,700 km (11,000 miles) across the Atlantic to the coast of Europe and then Africa down to the Antarctic.

❀ After a few months in the summer Antarctic, they begin the return journey to the Arctic. They probably see more daylight than any other animal.

❀ Considering that Arctic Terns fly at least 35,400 km (22,000 miles) each year and that they may live 10 or more years, they will have flown about 400,000 km (a quarter of a million miles) in their lifetime. The average human 'frequent flier' will have flown less than half that on commercial aircraft.

Arctic Terns migrate from the Arctic to the Antarctic – then back again!

UNCOMMON BEHAVIOUR

The male Common Tern flies with a fish in his bill, tempting a following female. When she catches up, he offers her the fish in midair. They both glide to the ground, where the male struts in front of the female. If she is interested in mating, she will come forward for the fish. Of course, there is sometimes the unscrupulous male who poses as a female in order to snag a free meal.

Crows vs Ravens

❖ Ravens are much larger than crows, although this can be hard to tell at a distance.

❖ It is easy to tell the difference during flight, because crows' tails are squared or rounded off, while ravens' are wedge-shaped.

a Common Raven – its size and tail shape distinguish it from a crow

What to Do About Birds as Garden Pests

1 Do not provide food or water.

2 Discourage nesting.

3 Cover vegetable plants and fruit trees with netting.

4 Hang mobiles, tape, tinsel, mylar or crepe paper.

5 Install scarecrows, plastic owls or snakes.

6 Do not trap, harass or harm them in any way without proper permits – migratory birds are protected by a number of international and domestic laws.

deter pest birds with a scarecrow

Pigeons vs Doves

❀ There is no real difference between pigeons and doves, although those birds called doves tend to be smaller.

❀ When the Normans invaded England in 1066 they introduced the word pigeon, while the Anglo Saxons called the same kind of bird a dove.

❀ The common urban bird most call a pigeon was once called the Rock Dove, now renamed Rock Pigeon.

❀ Pigeons and doves range in size from the 30 g (1 oz) Diamond Dove of Australia to the 2,000 g (70 oz) Blue Crowned Pigeon of New Guinea.

all those urban pigeons are part of the dove family

Snowy Owl

COURTSHIP FEEDING

The male Snowy Owl in tundra regions of the Arctic hunts for a lemming, catches it and lands on a mound of permafrost. He looks for a female and, with his wings displayed behind him like a cape, he offers her the food. The contrast between the dark brown rodent and snowy background serves to stimulate her interest.

Gay Gulls

Female-to-female bonding occurs in several species of gulls – up to 10 per cent of all pairs in Western Gull colonies. These pairings apparently are a result of a shortage of males. Even so, female–female pairings can produce young (after mating with males outside the nest site).

when males are scarce, girl gulls get together

Adaptations of Nest Parasites

❖ A protrusible cloaca (common urogenital opening) allows a nest parasite (a bird that lays its eggs in another bird's nest) to lay eggs in places that are too small for the adult parasite to enter.

❖ The eggs of nest parasites have thicker shells to prevent breakage because they are laid rapidly, perhaps only in a second or two.

❖ In about half of the nest-parasitic cuckoo species, the newly hatched cuckoo nestling gets under the host eggs or young and scoots them out over the rim of the nest so that only the cuckoo hatchling remains.

❖ A newly hatched cowbird, however, grows faster if it has competition from nest mates that are the young of the host species. A single young cowbird begs for food and gets its share if alone, but it gets more food if its nest mates help in the begging, even though they do not get a fair share of the food.

an adult Dunnock feeding a young cuckoo

THE SMELL OF DEATH

Ravens were once thought to have such a good sense of smell that they could smell impending death, so no one wanted to have these birds fly over their house.

BIRD SINGING COMPETITIONS

Competitions among songbirds are popular all over Indonesia, especially Bali, where few households are without a caged bird. An area is fenced off and a scaffold is erected from which many ornate birdcages are hung. When competition begins, the bird owners enter the area, pull the covering off the cages and urge their birds to sing. The judges walk up and down the aisles as the bird owners try to attract the judges' attention to their birds. The winners collect plastic trophies – the contest is not about money but prestige.

ducks quack louder in the city

ADAPTING TO NOISE

✿ The European Nightingale, in response to the increasing noise of European cities, has been upping the volume of its own song in order to attract a mate. The loudest recorded nightingale song was 95 decibels, loud enough to cause ear damage if the bird were sitting on your shoulder while singing.

✿ Ducks in the countryside quack with a slow drawl, while city ducks quack faster, more often and louder – like their human counterparts.

Fish Owls

Fish-eating owls typically swoop down to capture fish at or near the surface of a pond or lake, but some actually wade into shallow water to fish.

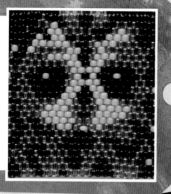

DECOY

Tame ducks were once used to attract wild ducks to hunting grounds; in Britain, they became known as decoys from the Dutch eendekooi, which means duck cage.

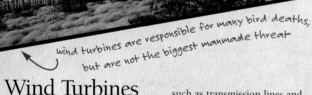

wind turbines are responsible for many bird deaths, but are not the biggest manmade threat

Wind Turbines

❖ Although wind turbines kill birds, the Royal Society for the Protection of Birds generally supports their use as alternative sources of energy; because global climatic changes are the greatest threat to birds, anything that can be done to decrease greenhouse gases will be beneficial.

❖ If properly placed – out of migratory pathways, for example – wind turbines are safer than many other large artificial structures, such as transmission lines and microwave towers.

❖ A Dutch study concluded that the 1,700 wind turbines in the Netherlands kill about 50,000 birds a year, while 2 million birds are killed by motor vehicles on the nation's roads. In the US, between 10,000 and 40,000 birds are killed annually by wind turbines, while 60–80 million are killed on the roads.

Feather Isotopes

Birds are what they eat, so the chemical composition of feathers reflects the food they gather in their habitat. Using this knowledge, scientists can determine where birds have nested and migrated by examining the isotopes of hydrogen in their feathers.

the Trumpet Manucode is one of 43 bird of paradise species

Birds of Paradise

✿ Having evolved on the isolated island of New Guinea, the 43 species of birds of paradise developed spectacular plumages and courtship behaviour to attract mates.

✿ Some male birds of paradise attract females by clearing an area of the forest floor to be used as a stage for their displays. The area, as much as 1 m (1 yd) in diameter, is so clean that if a leaf falls onto this stage, the bird will immediately fly down from his perch and remove it.

✿ Ornate feathers might be a handicap elsewhere, but New Guinea has few mammalian predators or competitors to eat their food, so the birds' outrageous colours and mating displays do not encumber them.

✿ Birds of paradise are so ornate that early ornithologists examining a stuffed specimen of one thought they were some practical joker's creation.

RSPB LOGO
The Royal Society for the Protection of Birds has as its logo the Pied Avocet, one of the first birds to symbolize conservation efforts in ornithology.

For parrot owners who want to prevent their parrots from flying off while out of their cage, leashes are available in appropriate sizes.

A FEATHER IN YOUR CAP

Today this phrase refers to an accomplishment. It originated from the practice of awarding a feather to a soldier who had killed an enemy.

ALBATROSS CAPITAL OF THE WORLD
There are 21 recognized species of albatrosses and 12 of them breed in New Zealand. Of these, seven breed only in New Zealand and nowhere else in the world.

a Wandering Albatross – endemic to New Zealand – doing its courtship dance

THE MISNAMED NIGHTHAWK:
THE NIGHTHAWK IS NEITHER NOCTURNAL NOR A HAWK.

the Northern Shoveler has a distinctive spoon-like bill

The Spoonbill

The Northern Shoveler, found both in the US and Europe, is unusual with its spatula-like bill, used to shovel through the mud and muck in search of invertebrates. Superficially resembling a Mallard with a spoon-like bill, it has earned the nicknames Spoonie, Hollywood Mallard, Smiling Mallard, Spadebill, Broadbill and Scopperbill.

Coordinated Hatching

In a number of species with large clutches and precocious young, such as partridges, quail, Mallards, and geese, it is important for all the young to hatch simultaneously so that the female does not have to incubate eggs and watch over young at the same time. It has been known for some time that young make 'pipping' sounds with their bill against the eggshell before hatching. It was thought that this was to communicate with the mother, but it may actually be a way for the unhatched young to communicate with each other and coordinate their hatching times.

a Mallard in flight

HUMMING A DIFFERENT TUNE

❖ In spite of their name, hummingbirds do not hum but make a whirring sound with their wings. Different species can be recognized by their individual wing sounds.

❖ Over 70 per cent of a hummingbird's wing is comprised of bones of the hand; the arm bones are considerably shortened.

❖ The average hummingbird beats its wings 25 times per second when flying; smaller hummingbirds may do so 80 times per second.

MOST TALKATIVE BIRDS

❖ An African Grey Parrot named Prudle had a vocabulary of nearly 1,000 human words, although it probably only understood what a few of them meant.

❖ Sparkie Williams, perhaps the most famous Budgerigar, could speak over 500 words and recite several short nursery rhymes. BBC's sound archive has his words preserved for posterity.

many parrots are great mimics

BIRDS IN SPORTS

New Zealand Kiwis	Cricket
Newcastle Falcons	Rugby
Norwich City Canaries	Football
Sheffield Wednesday Owls	Football
Crystal Palace Eagles	Football
Swansea City Swans	Football
Bristol City Robins	Football
Newcastle United Magpies	Football
Pittsburgh Penguins	Ice hockey
Atlanta Hawks	Basketball

the hummingbird's wings make a whirring sound, not a humming one

inside a one-day-old hen's egg

EGG-STRUCTION

The Church of San Francisco in Lima, Peru, contains the first cemetery of Lima – underground catacombs entombing 75,000 bodies. Constructed in the 1500s, the catacombs were made from calcium carbonate, sand and the whites of hundreds of thousands of seabird eggs.

What Is It Like Inside an Egg?

A developing bird is confined inside a shell for 14 to 60 days or more. How does it eat, breathe and get rid of wastes?

✿ The yolk of the egg is the nutrition, consisting of about 50 per cent water, 32 per cent fat, 16 per cent protein and 2 per cent carbohydrates.

✿ The shell has between 6,000 and 12,000 minute pores, so exchange of carbon dioxide and oxygen is easy.

✿ Waste products pose the most severe problem because accumulation of them could be toxic in this confined space. Instead, they are stored in a special membrane called the allantois until hatching.

EGG-ZPERIMENT

Bird eggs are stronger than they seem. Try this simple experiment, but put on an apron and do it over a sink just in case. Take off any rings you might have on your dominant hand and put a raw chicken egg into your palm. Squeeze as hard as you can. Most people cannot break the egg, demonstrating its sturdiness.

YOU MUST BE YOLK-ING

A kiwi's egg is 61 per cent yolk, almost twice that found in the eggs of precocial birds (those whose young hatch covered with down and able to feed on their own).

Basic White

All reptile eggs are white and their nests are hidden. Over time, birds developed different colours in order to camouflage their eggs against predation. This is substantiated by the following facts:

1 White eggs are almost always found in the nest of hole nesters, where camouflage is not that important.

2 White eggs are also produced by open nesters where incubation starts immediately and a parent always covers the eggs.

3 They are also found in open nests where eggs are covered with down or vegetation.

egg colour has no effect on the colour of chicks

eggs provide such high-quality protein that they are classified with meat in nutritional food groupings

Egg Sexing

It is important for chicken breeders to separate the sexes of newly hatched chickens. The technique of determining the sex of a newly hatched chicken by examining its vent (rear end) was developed by the Japanese. It is a difficult technique to learn and skilled egg sexers are paid well. There is even an Annual All-Japan Chick Sexing Championship where the record is 100 eggs in 3 minutes and 6 seconds. However, new breeds of chickens are being introduced whose eggs can be easily sexed by unskilled workers, making chicken egg sexing a dying art. A laboratory has also developed a technique to tell the sex of a newly hatched bird by using the tissue left in the eggshell after hatching.

crushed oyster shells have been used as a calcium supplement in Tree Swallow experiments

CALCIUM SUPPLEMENTS

❖ Tree Swallows get little calcium in their diets, even though it is needed for eggshell production. Experimenters added crushed oyster shells to some nest boxes of Tree Swallows just as nest building began. The females whose nest was supplemented began laying eggs sooner and had larger clutches with bigger babies.

❖ The calcium content of the four eggs a female sandpiper lays is greater than her total body calcium content. Some sandpipers eat lemming teeth as an additional source of calcium.

GREAT HEARING

Great Grey Owls' hearing is so acute that they can catch small mammals under a layer of snow simply by listening for their movements.

do YOU think it's scary?

painting of a Great Horned Owl

Scary Owls

❖ In Shetland, Scotland, crofters once thought that if a cow were frightened by an owl, it would produce bloody milk.

❖ It was once thought that an owl hooting among houses meant a girl had lost her virginity.

❖ A recent survey of Britons over the age of 15 found that 39 per cent of the respondents consider owls to be frightening.

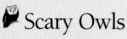

TAKES ONE TO KNOW ONE

Scrub Jays known to steal from the acorn caches of other Scrub Jays are careful about where they cache their own nuts. If they notice that they are being watched by other Scrub Jays while hiding their acorns, they will return later and rebury the nuts elsewhere.

PLANTS NAMED AFTER BIRDS

Gooseberry

Duckweed

Cuckoo Pint

Hen and Chickens

Cranesbill

Henbane

Bird-in-a-bush

Birdsfoot Trefoil

Storksbill

Hawksbeard

Pheasant's Eye

Crowfoot

Bird's-eye Speedwell

TALLEST BIRDS

❖ The tallest bird in Europe is the Common Crane at about 1.2 m (4 ft).

❖ The tallest bird in North America is the Whooping Crane at nearly 1.5 m (5 ft).

❖ The tallest flying bird in the world is the Sarus Crane at 1.7 m (5³/4 ft).

❖ The tallest non-flying bird in the world is the ostrich at 2.7 m (9 ft).

a nest parasite has added its egg to this nest – but humans shouldn't interfere

DON'T TOUCH A BIRD'S EGGS?

It has often been said that if one touches a bird's eggs or its nest, the bird will not return to the nest. This has not been substantiated and seems illogical because:

1 Most birds have a weak sense of smell and it seems unlikely that they would detect a human smell.

2 It seems more likely that they would try to protect rather than abandon their eggs or young if someone touched them.

put feeders around your garden to attract birds

MAKE YOUR GARDEN A BIRD SANCTUARY

1 Plant native vegetation for food and shelter.

2 Avoid the use of pesticides, herbicides or other chemicals.

3 Put up feeders in various locations.

4 Provide a water source with a pond, pool or birdbath.

5 Provide nest boxes for cavity nesters.

6 Keep your cat indoors.

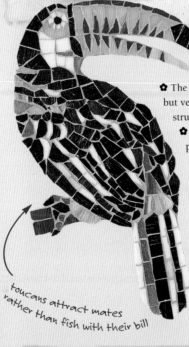

FISH-EATING TOUCANS?

✿ The colourful bill of the toucan is big but very light, with inner supporting struts of bone.

✿ The toucan uses its serrated bill to probe into dense vegetation after fruit, insects and small vertebrates such as lizards.

✿ The bill is colourful for the same reason most tropical birds are colourful – to attract mates.

✿ In the 1700s, when specimens of toucans were first seen in Europe, it was assumed that their bills evolved for catching fish rather than for eating fruit.

toucans attract mates rather than fish with their bill

SEEING RED

The Common Crane has a patch of red skin on its head that becomes bright red whenever the bird is excited or angry.

East German stamp featuring the Common Crane

feed avian visitors to your garden with foods such as sunflower seeds

NATIONAL BIRDS

list continues on page 53

Mute Swans were once known as 'royal birds'

The Swan and the Crown

For centuries, Mute Swans in Britain were harvested as a source of food. The swans were marked by registered nicks on their beaks to indicate ownership by important individuals. Any birds not marked were the property of the monarch and the swan became known as the 'royal bird'. Although they have not been eaten since the early 1900s, the tradition of marking swans is still practised by the Worshipful Companies of Vintners and Dyers on the River Thames in London, the only private owners of swans in Britain.

HUNTING WITH BOOMERANGS

❖ Birds were hunted with boomerangs by Australian Aborigines as far back as 10,000 years ago.

❖ Ancient Egyptians hunted ostriches and waterfowl in the same way – King Tut's tomb included a collection of boomerangs.

THE FIRST ENEMY AIRCRAFT SHOT DOWN IN WWII

This distinction belongs to a British aircraft called the Blackburn Skua, named after the predatory seabird. Skuas feed on the adults, young and eggs of various birds in far northern climes and are very defensive of their territory, dive bombing cattle, sheep, sheepdogs and people.

boomerangs were used to hunt birds in ancient times

BREAK AN EGG FOR LUCK?

In many cultures, throwing rice at weddings is a tradition. In France, the bride breaks an egg on the threshold of the new home before entering in order to ensure good luck and healthy babies.

crack an 'oeuf' for luck

GOOSE DERIVATIONS

The term 'goosing' has uncomfortable connotations. In the 1800s the terms 'gooser' and 'goose's neck' were nicknames for a man's penis. In the Elizabethan era, 'goose' was slang for a prostitute.

PAPER AIRPLANES

To demonstrate how birds glide, make a paper airplane of any style. Then modify its wings with flaps and folds to make it glide farther. What modifications are best? Can you launch one airplane farther than another? Which kind of airplanes and modifications are best for speed and which for gliding? Can an airplane be fast as well as glide far?

'goosing' has a history of sexual connotations

FAST FEEDERS: RAINBOW LORIKEETS HAVE BEEN TIMED FEEDING ON 35 EUCALYPTUS FLOWERS A MINUTE.

the Red-winged Blackbird sings 'oak-a-lee'

How Do Birds Learn to Sing?

Experimental studies have shown that songbirds' songs are both inherited and learned.

1 They inherit the basic core song, but the rest of the song is learned or refined by a newly hatched bird within about six weeks by listening to adults of the same species.

2 Young birds, as they practise their songs, learn more variations than they need and retain only some of them for later use. Which songs a young male bird keeps are influenced by the songs of his neighbours – he wants distinctive ones.

3 Birds raised in captivity that never hear the songs of the adults of their species learn a different kind of song, but with some inherited components.

the killdeer has zebra-like dark bands on its white breast as camouflage

🦩 Think of Zebras

Some ground-dwelling birds hide from potential predators by camouflaging themselves. The most obvious way is to blend into the background by having earth-tone plumage that mimics the ground, such as nightjars or many sandpipers. However, many wading birds have seemingly striking patterns, with bold stripes, bands or patches of black or brown on white bellies. This is also a form of camouflage called disruptive coloration. The patterning breaks up the outline of the bird and, when it is not moving, even strikingly patterned birds such as plovers are hard to see.

SNAIL FOOD

✿ Snails are the preferred food of African and Asian Openbill Storks. These birds have a bill that does not completely close; the tips touch but otherwise the top and bottom of the bill do not. One can see through the bill from one side to another. This unusual arrangement makes it easier to extract the snails from their shells.

✿ An unusual bird of aquatic habitats, the Limpkin feeds only on the right-handed apple snail. From numerous probes into the snail shells, the bill tip becomes noticeably bent to the right.

MUSICAL SCALES AND NOTES IN BIRD SONG

The Skylark is known for its beautiful song, but British musician David Hindley discovered that it is actually singing music. He recorded the Skylark's song and then slowed it down and discovered he could recognize individual notes. He extracted enough notes so that it could be played as human music; parts of it even resembled Beethoven's Fifth Symphony. Similarly, Hindley found that the song of the Woodlark resembles the structure of JS Bach's 48 Preludes and Fugues.

birds sing musical notes

JORDAN	Sinai Rosefinch
KOREA	Black-billed Magpie
LATVIA	White Wagtail
LIBERIA	Common Bulbul
LITHUANIA	White Stork
LUXEMBOURG	Goldcrest
MALAYSIA	Malaysian Peacock Pheasant
MALTA	Blue Rock Thrush
MARIANA ISLANDS	Guam Rail
MEXICO	Crested Caracara
MONTSERRAT	Montserrat Oriole
MYANMAR	Indian Peafowl
NORWAY	European Dipper
PALAU	Palau Fruit Dove
PANAMA	Harpy Eagle
PAPUA NEW GUINEA	Raggiana Bird of Paradise
PARAGUAY	Bare-throated Bellbird
PERU	Andean Cock-of-the-Rock
PHILIPPINES	Philippine Eagle
POLAND	White-tailed Sea Eagle
PUERTO RICO	Bananaquit
ST HELENA	Wirebird
ST KITTS AND NEVIS	Brown Pelican
ST VINCENT AND GRENADINES	St Vincent Parrot
SAO TOME AND PRINCIPE	African Grey Parrot
SINGAPORE	White-bellied Sea Eagle
SOUTH AFRICA	Blue Crane
SRI LANKA	Ceylon Jungle Fowl
SWAZILAND	Violet-crested Turaco
SWEDEN	Eurasian Blackbird
TAIWAN	Gray-faced Buzzard Eagle
THAILAND	Siamese Fireback Pheasant
TOBAGO	Scarlet Ibis
TRINIDAD	Scarlet Ibis
TURKEY	Redwing
UGANDA	Gray Crowned Crane
UNITED KINGDOM	European Robin
UNITED STATES	Bald Eagle
U.S. VIRGIN ISLANDS	Bananaquit
URUGUAY	Rufous Hornero
VENEZUELA	Troupial
ZAMBIA	African Fish Eagle
ZIMBABWE	African Fish Eagle

SHELLFISH ETIQUETTE

✿ The Pied-billed Grebe has a stouter bill than any other grebe, and its shape and strong jaw muscles enable the bird to catch crayfish. It holds the crayfish by one claw and shakes it until the claw detaches. Then it does the same for the other claw, after which it swallows the crayfish tail first.

✿ Oystercatchers are long-billed birds that eat a variety of foods but prefer shellfish. To access the shellfish innards, the bird has to sever the muscles that hold the shell together.

BUILD YOUR OWN BIRDHOUSE

A simple birdhouse can be constructed using an old milk carton in three easy steps.

1 Wash out the carton. Cut a 5 cm (2 in) hole in one side.

2 Seal the top with waterproof tape.

3 Use a piece of wire or cord to hang the birdhouse from a tree. Not only are you helping wildlife, but you are also reusing materials that otherwise would have gone into the garbage.

place a bird feeder in your garden as well as a birdhouse to attract lots of avian visitors

PEOPLE NAMED AFTER BIRDS: Robin, Jay, Martin, Phoebe

a Firewood Gatherer with its conspicuously large nest of sticks

🦤 Gathering Firewood?

A rather dull-looking bird, the Firewood Gatherer gets its name from the large nests it makes of sticks and places conspicuously on small trees or artificial structures such as telephone poles. The nests are dome- or cylinder-shaped, about 1 m (1 yd) high and have a side entrance near the top. The birds' nests have been known to cause fires by short-circuiting wires on power poles.

LEFT TO THEIR OWN DEVICES

❖ The male Brush Turkey and Malee Fowl of Australia build nests up to 4 m (13 ft) in diameter and 1 m (3 ft) high. Several females lay up to a total of 50 eggs in a nest.

❖ The eggs are incubated by the heat produced by the decomposing vegetation. The male keeps the nest at a constant temperature of 33–38°C (91–100°F) by inserting his bill into the mound to check the heat, then adding and removing plant matter as necessary.

❖ When the eggs hatch after approximately seven weeks, the hatchlings burrow out of the mound and are left to fend for themselves. They can easily do so because they are fully feathered and are able to fly just a few hours after hatching.

Brush Turkey

OBSOLETE BIRD NAMES

AMERICAN WIGEON – Once called Baldpate because of the white stripe on its head

MOORHEN – Water Hen

KESTREL – Called Wind Hover, because it hunts by hovering above the land

CORMORANT – Sea Crow

SHRIKE – Known as Butcherbird because it impales its prey on branches

BITTERN – Called Bull of the Mire, because of its low mooing sound

PEREGRINE – Duck Hawk

OSPREY – Fish Hawk, because it eats only fish

GREEN WOODPECKER – Named Yaffle, because of its loud, laughing call

OYSTERCATCHER – Sea Pie

REDSHANK – Watchdog of the Marshes, because it is the first wading bird to call when alarmed

GOLDEN EAGLE – Erne

WHIMBREL – Seven Whistler, because of its seven-note call

ALBATROSS – Gooney Bird, because of its awkward take-off

STORM PETREL – Mother Carey's Chicken

BLACK-NECKED STILT – Lawyer, apparently because of its formal-looking black-and-white plumage

CHOUGH – Red-legged Crow

FRIGATEBIRD – Man-O-War Bird, deriving from its piratical tendency of harassing other birds to drop the fish prey they have caught

BARN OWL – Screech Owl

THE MYSTERY OF THE ROC

The mythological Roc of Madagascar, said to eat elephants, is most likely based upon the Elephant Bird, 3.3 m (10 ft 8 in) tall and weighing 500 kg (1,100 lb). It became extinct around 1700.

Elephant Bird skeleton and egg

OLDEST STARLING: THE AVERAGE LIFESPAN OF THE EUROPEAN STARLING IS 2.5 YEARS, BUT THE LONGEVITY RECORD IS 22 YEARS.

take cover – I'm a messy eater

IL PENSEROSO

Sweet bird that shunn'st the noise of folly,
Most musical, most melancholy!

JOHN MILTON, 1632

EIGHT REASONS YOU MIGHT NOT WANT TO LIVE WITH A PARROT

1 They are loud.
2 They are messy.
3 They can bite.
4 They are destructive.
5 They are demanding and hard to care for and live with.
6 They can be expensive.
7 They can live for a long time.
8 Cute baby parrots grow up into less cute adults.

𓅪 Swallows vs Swifts

❀ The wings of a swift are thinner and more swept back than those of a swallow.
❀ A swift's wing beats seem more erratic than those of a swallow, almost as if the wings alternate flight beats.
❀ Some swifts have very short tails.

This Tree Swallow's wings distinguish it from the similar swift

MINIATURE SNOW SHOES

Grouse have special scales along either side of their toes in the winter to help them traverse snowy terrain.

ONLY SOME CANADA GEESE ARE CANADIAN

Canada Goose is the proper common name for the bird we are familiar with, but it is often erroneously called Canadian Goose. Some may be Canadian, but Canada Goose is their proper name.

EGG-ZACTLY RIGHT

✿ Some birds are termed determinate egg layers because they lay only a certain number of eggs and no more. The crow, Willow Ptarmigan, Budgerigar, Tricolored Blackbird and many wading birds are examples. If an egg is destroyed, the parent or parents will simply tend to whatever remains.

✿ Some birds are termed indeterminate egg layers, because after laying a clutch of eggs, if one is stolen or destroyed, the female will lay another in its place. Examples are Goldeneye ducks, California Quail, Cockatiels, coots and most fowl. In one experimental case where an egg was removed every day from a Northern Flicker's nest, the female flicker laid 71 eggs in 73 days.

The American Robin is a determinate egg layer, producing only 3-5 blue eggs

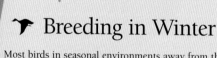

an Emperor Penguin with its young chick

🐦 Breeding in Winter

Most birds in seasonal environments away from the equator breed during the spring or autumn, whether in the northern or southern hemisphere. The Emperor Penguin, on the other hand, breeds during June and July in the Antarctic winter when the temperature drops to −40°C (−40°F). Two months of incubation under these harsh conditions are required, followed by three months of chick care. The reason for this schedule is that the chick, when it becomes independent, finds itself in the Antarctic summer when food is more abundant and the climate less harsh.

Bird Protection Act

The European Union's Directive on the conservation of wild birds sets out the modern framework for European states to take steps to protect migratory birds and birds of special conservation importance. In the UK, the response to the EU Directive was to revise bird protection within the Wildlife and Countryside Act of 1981. The Act makes it illegal to intentionally take, kill or injure wild birds, to take or destroy active nests, or to take eggs from them.

SHRINK YOUR PARROT?

For badly behaving pet birds there are now professional avian behaviour consultants who will help you work out problems that you and your avian bad boy are facing.

the patches on the Sunbittern's wings look like threatening eyes to predators

THERE IS A LESSON HERE
In England, 75 per cent of the land is farmed. There are 25 per cent more birds on the edges of organic farms.

The Starling Experiment

Starlings breeding in The Hague, Netherlands, fly southwestwards to winter in northern France and Britain. In the autumn of 1958, a Dutch biologist, AC Perdeck, captured a number of adult and immature starlings, ringed them and took them to Switzerland. When released, the adult starlings headed southwestwards but then changed course so that they arrived at their usual wintering grounds. Immature starlings, however, took the same course from Switzerland and ended up in central and southern France and even Spain. This shows that the basic migratory map is genetic but learning and maturity are required to make adjustments.

✦ young starling   ✦ adult starling

37 new bird species have been introduced on Hawaii

ISLAND INTRODUCTIONS

Exotic bird species introduced onto islands often overwhelm the natives. On Hawaii, with 37 introduced species, and Puerto Rico with 19, for example, exotic songbird species outnumber native ones.

POWDER DOWN

Among the other feathers of the body, parrots, pigeons and especially herons possess a particular kind of feather called powder down. The tips of these feathers break off, producing fine granules like talcum powder. Apparently this powder, like talcum powder, helps to waterproof the feathers.

WHY MOULT?

Most birds shed their feathers and grow new ones regularly because:

1 Feathers wear out and new ones are needed to replace them.

2 Old feathers might be infested with parasites.

3 Plumage may be changed to suit the season, with winter plumage often being dull or cryptically coloured to fool predators, and breeding plumage more colourful to attract females and deter competing males.

PLANTING YOUR GARDEN TO ATTRACT BIRDS

1 Choose a variety of vegetation, both in terms of species and structure.

2 Choose plants that birds can use for both shelter and food, but avoid invasive and alien species.

3 Provide a diverse mixture of food – berries, seeds, nuts and so on.

4 Select plants that will bear food at different times of year.

5 Shrubbery is the most important vegetation because it is so versatile.

plant your garden with a variety of berries and seeds to attract birds

BIRD FLIGHT SUITS

For those who let their pet birds roam around the house – soft, stretchable, reusable nappies can prevent those annoying accidents.

parrots, such as this military macaw, can suffer from the illness psittacosis

➤ Parrot Fever

❖ Psittacosis (now called ornithosis) is an illness with symptoms of fever, chills, headache, sensitivity to light, coughing and muscular aches. It is caused by the bacterium *Chlamydia psittaci*.

❖ Parakeets, parrots and love birds are most commonly infected, but other birds such as poultry, pigeons, canaries and seabirds may also be infected. Birds that are infected may not show symptoms.

❖ Humans become infected with psittacosis when they breathe in the bacteria that are present in dried bird droppings, feather dust or other secretions of infected birds.

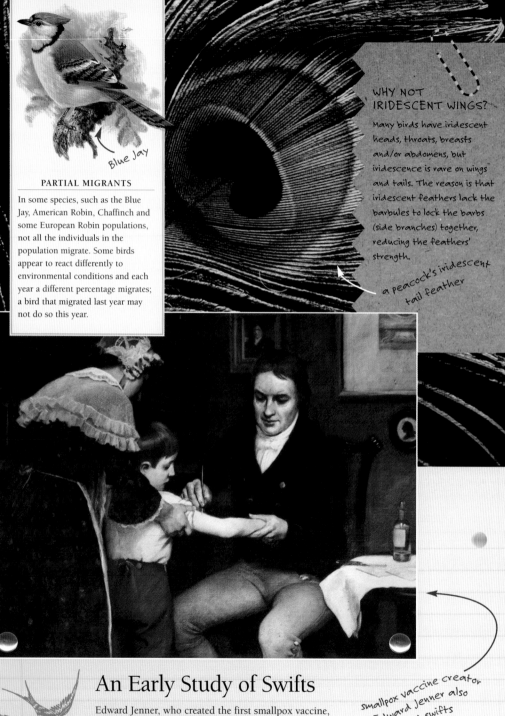

Blue Jay

PARTIAL MIGRANTS

In some species, such as the Blue Jay, American Robin, Chaffinch and some European Robin populations, not all the individuals in the population migrate. Some birds appear to react differently to environmental conditions and each year a different percentage migrates; a bird that migrated last year may not do so this year.

WHY NOT IRIDESCENT WINGS?

Many birds have iridescent heads, throats, breasts and/or abdomens, but iridescence is rare on wings and tails. The reason is that iridescent feathers lack the barbules to lock the barbs (side branches) together, reducing the feathers' strength.

a peacock's iridescent tail feather

An Early Study of Swifts

Edward Jenner, who created the first smallpox vaccine, also studied swifts in Gloucestershire, England; he caught 12 of them and clipped their toes so as to recognize them if captured again. Seven years later one of his cats brought one of these swifts home.

smallpox vaccine creator Edward Jenner also studied swifts

BIRD CALLS HAVE MEANING

A study of Black-capped Chickadees in which their calls were recorded, modified and played back to wild birds produced the following results:

✿ If the pitch increased (higher voice), the birds responded normally.

✿ If the pitch decreased, the birds ignored it (scientists speculate it is because the bird thinks the calling bird is much bigger).

✿ If the spaces between phrases were shortened, the birds reacted normally.

✿ If the time between phrases was lengthened, the birds ignored the song.

These changes were undetectable by the human ear, demonstrating the acute hearing ability of the birds' ears.

Red-billed Oxpeckers hitching a ride on the back of an antelope

➤ Oxpeckers

Oxpeckers are African birds that feed on the backs and necks of large mammals such as giraffes, rhinos, cape buffalo and antelopes. The birds eat parasites such as ticks, so are also called Tickbirds, and are apparently helpful to these large mammals. They also eat dead skin, saliva, blood, sweat and tears. Recent studies indicate that blood may be more important to the birds' diet than the ticks, and that tick removal from the large mammals may not be all that significant. It may simply be a strategy to fool the mammals into allowing the birds on their backs and necks.

RICH NEIGHBOURHOODS, RICHER BIRDS

A study of bird populations in the neighbourhood parks near Phoenix, Arizona, in the southwestern US showed that more birds of more species are present in more economically well-to-do neighbourhoods. The parks were comparable in structure, number of trees and so on, and the researchers do not have a clear explanation as yet.

Chairman Mao's attempts to rid China of sparrows contributed to widespread famine

Chairman Mao's 'War on the Sparrows'

In 1958 Chairman Mao decided to rid China of sparrows to save grain crops, enlisting country peasants to go into the field and scare the sparrows so that the birds would not land and would eventually die. The plan worked; the ground was littered with sparrow corpses and peasants proudly had their photos taken next to large piles of sparrow bodies. The next year the grain harvest was greatly increased. However, sparrows not only eat grain, but also the insects that eat grain. The following year a locust plague devastated the grain and, at least partially due to the war on sparrows, the country plunged into a famine.

THE RED CANARY

In the early twentieth century, canaries were very popular. Wild canaries are green birds, but in the late nineteenth century English canary breeders fed the birds red peppers to turn them orange. Of course, this is not genetic and not passed on to the offspring. In the 1930s, however, a red canary was produced by crossing the Black-hooded Siskin, a red-and-black bird, with a green canary, a close relative.

GLOBAL NAMES FOR THE HOUSE SPARROW

Moineau doméstique (French)

Gorrión doméstico (Spanish)

Haussperling (German)

Gråspurv (Danish)

Passera europea (Italian)

Wróbel (Polish)

Iesuzume (Japanese)

Huismus (Dutch)

Pardal (Portuguese)

Caption along photo edge: The Brown Tree Snake has caused the extinction of several bird species on the island of Guam

EIGHTEENTH-CENTURY MEDICINAL FOLKLORE

❖ Eagle's flesh was used to treat gout; the brain drunk in wine for jaundice; and the gallbladder used for diseases of the eyes.

❖ Osprey beaks were used to ease toothache by picking the gums with them until the gums bled.

❖ Goose fat was believed to cure baldness and help deafness, palsy, lameness and cramps.

❖ The oil gland of the ibis was used as a lip balm.

❖ The ashes of a raven were thought to cure epilepsy and gout.

❖ The droppings of a canary were used to cure the bite of a mad dog.

❖ Stuttering was supposedly cured by eating the eggs of a mockingbird.

❖ The blood of a lark, drunk with vinegar, was used to dissolve gallstones.

➤ Birds of Guam

The Mariana Fruit Dove, Guam Flycatcher, Rufous Fantail, Cardinal Honeyeater and other native birds of Guam have become extinct since the late 1940s, when the Brown Tree Snake began to colonize the island. These snakes are native to New Guinea, northern Australia, eastern Malaysia and the Solomon Islands and may have arrived with timber shipments during the WWII rebuilding efforts. Since the snake had no predators, its numbers increased exponentially.

Boy, That Water Is Cold!

Birds that spend a lot of time standing in cold water or damp environments have countercurrent circulation to reduce loss of body heat. Blood coming from the heart through the arteries is warm, while blood returning from the legs is cool. In order to avoid cooler blood entering the body on its way back to the heart, there is a 'heat exchanger' network of arteries and veins that closely intermingle. As the cooler blood passes from the feet and legs to the body, it is warmed by the warmer blood flowing out from the heart. Were it not for this system, the entire body would be cooled.

Canada Geese navigate by the stars in the night sky →

▼ Stellar Navigation

Many birds use the stars to navigate on their migratory journey.

✿ Ducks will fly aimlessly on a cloudy night until they break through the clouds into a clear sky and will then head in the proper direction. If the moon is so bright that the stars cannot be seen, they are unable to navigate.

✿ In the 1950s, German ornithologists Franz and Eleanore Sauer put caged European Warblers in a planetarium at the time of autumn migration. The warblers oriented themselves in their cages in a particular direction and the night sky was moved in that direction. This was repeated each night for several weeks. The warblers' 'virtual migration' showed that they followed the exact path that they would have followed had they been free to do so, travelling from Europe to Africa and even navigating around the Mediterranean. This was some of the first good evidence that birds used the star map as a guide on their migration.

BEAK EXCHANGE

All beaks come from similar tissues in bird embryos, so scientists took 36-hour-old duck and quail embryos from an incubator and drilled small holes in the eggs around them. Using tiny needles, the scientists switched certain cells between embryos. As a result, the ducks grew pointy little quail beaks and the quails grew flat, wide duck beaks. Understanding what causes a beak to develop could shed light on human facial development.

the same embryonic tissues produce many types of bird beak ↱

OLD OWL NAMES

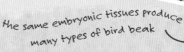

- In Old Norse, an owl was called ugla.
- In Old German, it was known as uwila.
- In Old English, it was ule.
- In Middle English, it was called owle.

help your wooden nestbox last longer by treating it with an appropriate paint or preservative

NESTBOX TIPS

❖ Put a nestbox in place well before the nesting season begins in the spring; birds may roost in it.

❖ Place nestboxes on the top of a sturdy pole or post facing parallel to the prevailing wind. Make sure the hole faces in any direction except south in the northern hemisphere, or north in the southern hemisphere, or it will be too hot for the young birds in summer.

❖ Nestboxes are best made of wood and are thus subject to the wear and tear of the weather and should be treated for longer lifetimes. Use a non-toxic, non-lead-based paint or preservative such as linseed oil. Paint only the outside – young birds will peck at the inside walls and eat some of the wood fibres. Paint or stain the box a natural colour to match the habitat and be less noticeable to predators.

❖ Clean the nestbox at the end of each season; a hinged roof makes that easier.

❖ Use the appropriate hole size and place the nestboxes in the appropriate habitat for the birds you want to attract. Place them at least 7.6 m (25 ft) apart.

TOWER BIRDS

King Charles II deemed that there must always be six ravens at the Tower of London and thus ravens have roamed the grounds of the tower for 350 years as a symbol of the monarchy's health. As legend has it, if the ravens leave the tower or die, the kingdom will fall. Successive ravens have faced a number of hazards over the years, including WWII bombings, freezing weather and more recently the threat of avian flu – and, of course, they have their wings clipped to prevent them from flying away.

ROOSTING

In the evening large flocks of starlings, swallows, martins and other species choose to sleep together in reed beds, shrubs and trees, most likely to provide more eyes for predator detection.

six ravens must be kept at the Tower of London or the British monarchy will fall

this is a boy budgie

HOW TO TELL A BOY BUDGIE FROM A GIRL

A budgie's sex is determined by the colour of its cere, the fleshy structure at the base of the upper beak around the nostrils. Adult males have a bluish cere and females' vary from pink to tan or brown.

LARGEST FAMILY OF BIRD SPECIES

Tyrant flycatchers are the largest family of birds with the greatest number of species (310).

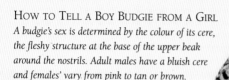

ACCIDENTAL COLONIZATION

In 1937, on their migration across the North Sea, a flock of Fieldfares was waylaid by a storm and blown to Greenland, where they became established as a non-migratory population.

THE BIG GUY: THE LARGEST PERCHING BIRD, OR PASSERINE, IS THE RAVEN AT ABOUT 1.5 KG (3 LBS).

the Canada Goose can maintain its course and speed despite adverse winds

Windage

Although birds do occasionally drift or get blown off course by the wind, studies of radio-tagged Canada Geese demonstrated that they are able to maintain a constant ground speed as well as a straight track over the ground by compensating for changes in the wind direction and speed.

NESTBOX BREEDERS

Here are some of the birds that will nest in nestboxes:

Wood Ducks

Goldeneyes

Buffleheads

Hooded Mergansers

Goosanders

Red-breasted Mergansers

Ural Owls

Pygmy Owls

Tawny Owls

Tengmalm's Owls

Kestrels

Woodpeckers

Stock Doves

Jackdaws

Tree Swallows

House Martins

Tits

Swifts

Nuthatches

Wrens

Bluebirds

European Starlings

House Sparrows

Tree Sparrows

Flycatchers

Robins

INFECTIOUS DISEASES OF GARDEN BIRDS

❖ Salmonellosis

❖ Colibacillosis

❖ Yersiniosis

❖ Pasteurellosis

❖ Chlamydiosis (also known as ornithosis or psittacosis)

❖ Trichomoniasis

❖ Avian pox

❖ Aspergillosis

STOOL PIGEON

❖ This designation derives from the French *estale* or *estal*, referring to a pigeon used to lure a hawk into a net.

❖ The French word may have originally come from the Germanic word *stall*, meaning a place or standing position.

❖ Today, a stool pigeon is a decoy or informer used to catch criminals.

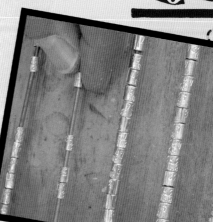

rings used for tracking migrating birds

🐦 Ringing/Banding

Ringing or banding involves attaching a ring or band to the leg of a bird to identify it. Because ringing birds requires capturing the birds and handling them before the ringing takes place, the ringing of birds in the UK is controlled under the Wildlife and Countryside Act of 1981 and organized by the British Trust for Ornithology (BTO). Official BTO rings may be placed on birds, by qualified ringers with permits; the BTO supervise the permit system. Ringing in the United States is controlled under the Migratory Bird Treaty Act and requires a federal permit. Some states require a state permit as well. Only official federal rings may be legally placed on birds that are released to the wild.

LONGEST BIRD PENIS

Most birds do not have a penis, but waterfowl and a few others do. The Argentine Lake Duck has a penis 42.5 cm (16³/₄ in) long – nearly as long as its body.

recreational egg hunting harms bird populations

The Oologist

In the nineteenth century, bird egg collecting for both scientific and recreational purposes was popular. Individuals, and groups like Boy Scout troops, would collect, trade and display eggs, much as we do stamps and coins today. A journal for collectors, *The Oologist*, reported on these activities and offered eggs for sale and trade. However, by the latter part of that century, it was beginning to be recognized that recreational egg hunting was adversely affecting bird populations. The eggs of the Labrador Duck were collected in large quantities in Quebec and Labrador and the population declined until the bird went extinct in the 1870s. Today, stealing birds' eggs is illegal.

young birds' mouth markings and begging behaviour elicit food

PRIMPING AND PREENING

Birds constantly run their beaks over their feathers to make sure that all the barbs of each feather are zipped together. Almost all birds possess a pair of preen glands on the top side of the tail called uropygial glands. These glands produce a mixture of fat, oil and wax. To help in waterproofing and moisturizing their feathers, and maybe as a parasite deterrent, birds use their beaks to squeeze this lotion from their preen glands and distribute it over their feathers.

most birds have preen glands on the top side of their tails

GAPE MARKS

Many young birds have distinctive markings in their mouth – on their tongue, palate and edges of their bill – some quite colourful and striking. These gape marks, along with begging behaviour, induce the parent to feed the young.

long-tailed bird bauble

a peacock's iridescent colours are the result of the way in which lightwaves pass through or reflect off them

the toucan's huge bill weighs less than the bird's feathers

LIGHT AS A FEATHER

It depends on the bird, but outside of the migratory season (when birds put on extra fat stores for energy), a bird's weight is generally distributed as follows:

1 Feathers comprise about 25 per cent of a bird's weight.

2 A bird has approximately 175 muscles, constituting about 50 per cent of its weight. About half the muscles' weight is in the flight muscles – the pectoralis and suprocoracoideus (breast muscles).

3 The remaining 25 per cent of a bird's weight is made up by the organs, blood and the skeleton.

FEATHER COLOURS

✿ The colours of feathers are produced in two ways: pigment and structure.

✿ Brown, grey, yellow, black, tan, orange and related colours are caused by pigments in the feathers.

✿ The turaco family of Africa contains red and green copper pigments found in no other animal. In other birds, different pigments combined with light refraction produce such colours.

✿ Bluebird blue, parrot green, white, metallic red and iridescence are produced by the structure of the feather. To produce blue colour, brown granules in the barbs of the feather scatter light – red and yellow wavelengths pass through the granules, while blue is reflected.

✿ If you find a feather from a blue bird – a jay, Blue Tit or kingfisher, for example – look at the feather in your hand; it will appear blue. Then hold the feather up to the light and look through it; it will appear brown.

woodcut illustration of a grebe from
Conrad Gesner's sixteenth-century
Historiae Animalium (Studies on Animals)

➤ Feather Eating

Grebes are the only birds that eat their own
feathers, usually plucked from the breast and
abdomen areas. The feathers ball up in the
stomach, where they are partially digested and
mixed with food, making a bolus of food and
feathers that is eventually regurgitated. This habit
apparently serves to protect the intestine from hard-
to-digest fish bones. Parents even feed feathers to
their newborn chicks.

LIGHTEST AND HEAVIEST FEATHERS

✿ The lightest feathers on a bird are called filoplumes.
Found over the skin of a bird, a hundred of them might
weigh just 1 g ($^1/_{32}$ oz). Filoplumes might have a function
in sensing the position of other feathers as a bird moves.
✿ The heaviest feathers on a bird are the flight feathers
on the wings – the primaries on the outer wing that effect
propulsion, and the secondaries on the inner wing that
produce lift. Their shaft is thick and stiff to withstand the
pressures of beating the air. All the primary feathers
together weigh as much as all the body feathers of a bird.

ALBINO PEACOCK? WITH BLUE EYES
RATHER THAN PINK, THE WHITE
PEACOCK IS NOT ACTUALLY AN
ALBINO, BUT A WHITE VARIETY
OF THE BLUE INDIAN PEACOCK.

XYZ

Mammals, including humans, have X and Y chromosomes, XX indicating female and XY indicating male. Birds have W and Z chromosomes, the female having WZ and the male ZZ.

Bald Eagle Alaska

About half of the world's 70,000 Bald Eagles live in Alaska. More than 100,000 Bald Eagles were killed in Alaska from 1917 to 1953 because fishermen thought they threatened the salmon population.

the biggest population of Bald Eagles lives in Alaska

BIRDY SAYINGS

A bird's-eye view.

A little bird told me.

That's for the birds.

He flew the coop.

Feather your nest.

Eat like a bird.

Free as a bird.

Sitting duck.

A lame duck.

Scarcer than hen's teeth.

Madder than a wet hen.

Out on a lark.

A feather in your cap.

Something to crow about.

Wise as an owl.

Watch like a hawk.

As the crow flies.

Your goose is cooked.

Naked as a jay bird.

Voice like a nightingale.

Eagle eye.

Night owl.

Booby hatch.

Sitting in the catbird seat.

Like the cat who swallowed the canary.

MIGRATION ALTITUDES

Tracking birds with radar has demonstrated that 95 per cent of migratory movements occur at less than 3,000 m (10,000 ft), with most birds flying under 915 m (3,000 ft).

🦅 Hammerhead

✿ The Hamerkop (Afrikaans for 'Hammerhead'), native to southern and central Africa, is well known for its enormous nest – a tri-level structure up to 2 m (2 yds) high and 2 m (2 yds) wide, weighing nearly 50 kg (110 lb).

✿ Constructed of sticks and mud, the nest may be comprised of 8,000 individual pieces, and is topped with a roof adorned with an array of objects – from feathers and snake skins to various manmade items.

✿ The nest is strong enough to withstand the weight of a man – quite an accomplishment for the smallest stork on the continent.

✿ A Hamerkop pair may build 3–5 nests per year, rarely staying in one nest for more than a few months. Apparently the purpose of all the nest building is simply to cement the pair's bond.

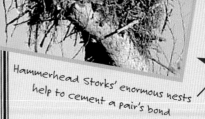

Hammerhead Storks' enormous nests help to cement a pair's bond

a painting of Great Auks by nineteenth-century ornithologist John James Audubon

THE GREAT AUK

In some ways a symbol for the extinction of birds, the flightless Great Auk, resembling a penguin, became extinct on 3 June 1844, because of collectors. Two adult Great Auks on Eldey Island, Iceland, were caught and killed, one story having it that a third collector was disappointed that he did not get to club one. The adults were incubating an egg – probably the last egg ever laid by this species.

EGG SHAPES

❖ Birds' eggs come in different shapes. Some are more pointed, while others are more rounded. The shape is determined by the internal structure of the female.

❖ Aristotle stated that eggs that tapered to a point produced females and the rounder ones produced males. This is not true.

❖ The typical egg shape is somewhat modified by environmental conditions. For example, the several species of seabird called murres lay their eggs on narrow cliff ledges. The eggs are very pointed at one end, like a triangle; if bumped, an egg is more likely to roll in a tight arc than roll off the cliff.

❖ Rather than having a large and small end like most eggs, the emu's egg is tapered at both ends.

quail's egg

Social weavers nest in large colonies to foil predators

Nesting in Colonies

One reason for nesting or roosting in large colonies, such as those of seabirds, is to overwhelm the predators in the area. The larger the colony, the smaller the proportion of birds that will be eaten by predators. Social weavers of Africa cooperate to build a large colonial nest that helps protect them against predators and the hot climate. These nests are so substantial that they may be used for a hundred or more generations.

HOW DO HUMMINGBIRDS HOVER?

For many years it was assumed that hummingbirds hover by producing equal lift from both the upstroke and downstroke of their wings. However, sophisticated equipment and very high-speed photography of a hummingbird hovering in a wind tunnel in an atmosphere of very fine olive oil droplets showed that the downstroke provided 75 per cent of the lift.

BETTER THAN RADAR Western Grebes, wintering on the ocean, feed at night using the phosphorescent trails left by fish in the water through bioluminescent plankton.

the downstroke of the wings provides most of the lift that enables hummingbirds to hover

No Weight Watchers

✿ Waders or shorebirds, among the longest of migrants, prepare for the migration by increasing the size of their flight muscles and putting on lots of body fat.

✿ Fat may make up one third to one half of a migratory wader's body weight. The Sanderling, for example, may double its weight from 60 to 120 g (2 to 4 oz) before migration, most of the weight being fat stores.

✿ The extra fat provides energy for the journey, which is often many thousands of kilometres or miles.

ANT FOLLOWERS

There are some 200 species of antbirds in the New World tropics. All eat mainly arthropods and a few are found exclusively in association with army ant swarms. The birds eat the arthropods that are flushed by the marauding swarms of ants as they move through the forest. These neotropical army ants are similar to African driver ants in that both have birds that subsist by capturing arthropods escaping from the ants.

SEVEN SIGNS OF ILLNESS IN A PET BIRD

1 Fluffed up

2 Loss of appetite

3 Weight loss

4 Change in appearance of droppings

5 Runny nostrils or eyes

6 Droopy wings

7 Sleeps a lot

a pair of healthy pet finches in their birdcage

QUIET VULTURES

Vultures lack a syrinx, the sound-producing organ that most birds have, so they are nearly silent, although they can produce hissing and wheezing sounds when disturbed.

if you're looking for the strong, silent type, I'm the Egyptian Vulture for you

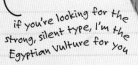

NORTH PACIFIC

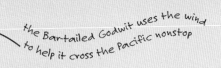

▼ Longest Nonstop Migration

The Bar-tailed Godwit is a large wading bird that breeds in Alaska and flies nonstop from western Alaska across the Pacific Ocean, over 11,000 km (nearly 7,000 miles), to New Zealand and Australia. The bird is unable to land on the sea, so this long migration involves a 4–5 day nonstop flight. One reason the bird is able to accomplish this longest of all nonstop migrations is that its migration is timed to take advantage of winds of 112–145 kph (70–90 mph) from the north that develop over the Aleutian Islands, which give it a strong start on this amazing journey.

SOUTH PACIFIC

MOST ABUNDANT BIRD: ONE OF THE BEST CANDIDATES FOR THIS TITLE IS THE RED-BILLED QUELEA OF AFRICA, WITH A BREEDING POPULATION OF 1.5 BILLION.

ANOTHER LINK TO REPTILES

Birds have a highly vascularized (contains many blood vessels) structure called pecten in their eye that reptiles, but not mammals, also possess. This highly folded fan-like structure extending from the retina apparently serves to provide nutrients to the eye. Predatory birds such as eagles have the largest pecten.

WHY DO BIRDS STAND ON ONE LEG?

If they lifted it up, they would fall down ... but the real reason is to conserve body heat. This is especially true with wading birds standing in cool or cold water. Tucking the leg up into the body feathers saves energy. For the same reason, some waders and ducks will turn their head and tuck their bill under the feathers on their back or wing. Grebes can actually put their legs onto their back and under the wings as they float on water.

standing on one leg helps
these Canada Geese
to conserve body heat

THE EGG-BALANCING MYTH

It has been said that eggs can be easily balanced on their wide end only on the vernal equinox. Not only does this conflict with the laws of astronomy and physics, but Phil Spott broke the world record by balancing 439 eggs at the same time and it was not the equinox.

FOR SPEED AND ENDURANCE

Hopi Indians tied roadrunner feathers to the tails of their horses to ensure speed and endurance.

RADIATOR BEHAVIOUR

During periods of extreme heat, roadrunners of the arid southwestern US squat on the ground with their wings spread and the outer layer of feathers lifted to allow circulation of air for cooling.

beep-beep, beep-beep, beep-beep

The Birds

Alfred Hitchcock's movie *The Birds* showed thousands of birds attacking humans. The director supposedly was inspired by a 1961 incident in which seabirds attacked the terrified residents of Monterey Bay in California. Recent research has shown that the birds were suffering the effects of ingesting contaminated plankton.

Alfred Hitchcock's movie The Birds was inspired by real-life bird attacks in California

TRADITIONAL BIRD CLASSIFICATION

Struthioniformes Ostrich, emus, kiwis and allies

Tinamiformes Tinamous

Anseriformes Waterfowl

Galliformes Pheasants and allies

Gaviiformes Loons or divers

Podicipediformes Grebes

Procellariiformes Albatrosses, petrels and allies

Sphenisciformes Penguins

Pelecaniformes Pelicans and allies

Ciconiiformes Storks and allies

Phoenicopteriformes Flamingos

Accipitriformes Eagles, hawks and allies

Falconiformes Falcons

Turniciformes Button-quail

Gruiformes Cranes and allies

Charadriiformes Plovers and allies

Pteroclidiformes Sandgrouse

Columbiformes Pigeons and doves

Psittaciformes Parrots and allies

list continues on page 78

Egyptian pyramid builders may have eaten mass-produced chickens

Egyptian Incubators

In the fourth century BC, Egyptians began to mass-produce chickens, perhaps to feed all those who worked on the pyramids. They invented the process of artificial incubation and produced 15–20 million young birds each year.

Seven Tips for Setting Up a Bird Feeder

1 Use different feeders with different foods to attract different birds; it is especially important to separate large and small birds.

2 Place the feeder where it can be seen from the house, but not too close, especially to the windows.

3 Place it near bushes, hedges or trees where birds can retreat quickly if they perceive danger.

4 Place it high enough so that domestic or feral cats will have difficulty reaching it.

5 Plant seed-bearing plants such as sunflowers and zinnias near the feeder to attract birds.

6 A source of water nearby is important.

7 Keep the bird feeder clean and the food dry.

ANI EATER

Groove-billed Anis of Central America, 30 cm (12 in) long and relatives of the cuckoo, are preyed upon by carnivorous bats.

THE FIRST BIRD FEEDER

In the nineteenth century, an English ornithologist by the name of Dovaston set up the first bird feeders outside his window. These feeders eventually fed 23 species of birds.

tube-style bird feeder

traditional bird classification – list continued from page 77

Cuculiformes Cuckoos

Strigiformes Owls

Caprimulgiformes Nightjars and allies

Apodiformes Swifts

Trochiliformes Hummingbirds

Coraciiformes Kingfishers and allies

Piciformes Woodpeckers and allies

Trogoniformes Trogons

Coliiformes Mousebirds

Passeriformes Passerines or perching birds

KIWIS

The kiwis of New Zealand are strange birds. Being nocturnal, they do not see well, but their hearing and sense of smell are acute. Their ears are well developed and their sensitive nose consists of nostrils at the tip of an 18 cm (7 in) bill that the birds use to probe and sniff out worms. Once located, kiwis pick up their prey as if using tweezers. The long bristles, called rictal bristles, on the side of the bill may serve as feelers.

the kiwi's nostrils are at the end of its bill – very unusual for a bird

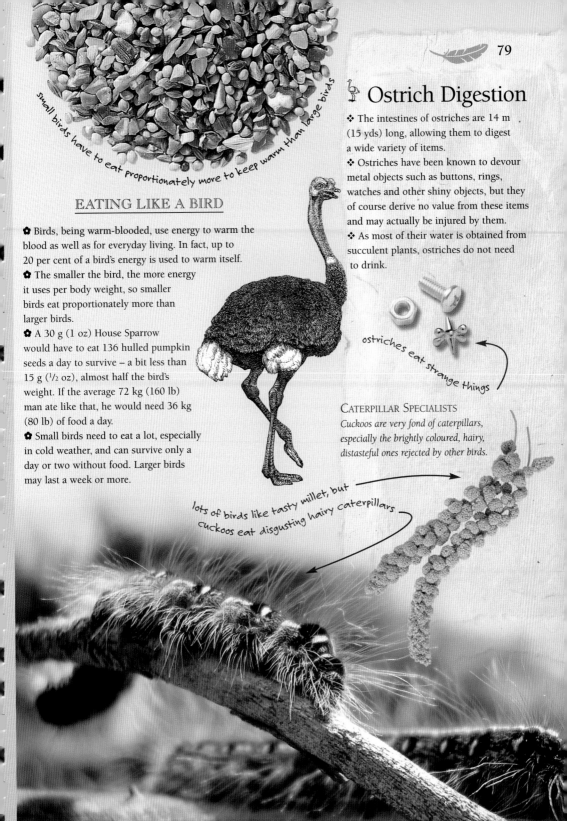

small birds have to eat proportionately more to keep warm than large birds

EATING LIKE A BIRD

✿ Birds, being warm-blooded, use energy to warm the blood as well as for everyday living. In fact, up to 20 per cent of a bird's energy is used to warm itself.

✿ The smaller the bird, the more energy it uses per body weight, so smaller birds eat proportionately more than larger birds.

✿ A 30 g (1 oz) House Sparrow would have to eat 136 hulled pumpkin seeds a day to survive – a bit less than 15 g (¹/₂ oz), almost half the bird's weight. If the average 72 kg (160 lb) man ate like that, he would need 36 kg (80 lb) of food a day.

✿ Small birds need to eat a lot, especially in cold weather, and can survive only a day or two without food. Larger birds may last a week or more.

♃ Ostrich Digestion

❖ The intestines of ostriches are 14 m (15 yds) long, allowing them to digest a wide variety of items.

❖ Ostriches have been known to devour metal objects such as buttons, rings, watches and other shiny objects, but they of course derive no value from these items and may actually be injured by them.

❖ As most of their water is obtained from succulent plants, ostriches do not need to drink.

ostriches eat strange things

CATERPILLAR SPECIALISTS

Cuckoos are very fond of caterpillars, especially the brightly coloured, hairy, distasteful ones rejected by other birds.

lots of birds like tasty millet, but cuckoos eat disgusting hairy caterpillars

FISH DROWNS BIRD

Osprey are known for their ability to catch fish. Their claws are so long that the bird cannot walk on land, but they allow the bird to get a strong hold on its piscine prey. The bird also has prickles on the bottom of its feet to help grip onto slippery fish. One time a carp in a lake in Germany was found with the skeleton of one of these birds imbedded in its flesh.

'fly-fisher' extraordinaire – an Opsrey with its catch

BIRD-FRIENDLY COFFEE

Coffee has been traditionally grown in the shade of other trees in the tropical forest, but newer coffee plantations are grown in the sun for a higher yield. These provide less habitat for birds. Shade-grown coffee plantations, more like native forests, are important in the protection of both resident and migratory birds.

PLANTS POISONOUS TO PET BIRDS

Any flowers that grow from bulbs

Amaryllis

Apple seeds

Apricot and peach pits

Dieffenbachia

Hydrangea

Iris

Ivy

Oleander

Philodendron

Poinsettia

Potatoes

Rhubarb

eighteenth-century picture of a cockfight

Cockfighting

Cockfighting is a sport in which two or more specially bred birds are placed in an enclosure to fight, mainly for gambling and entertainment, although the original reason was to serve as an alternative to battle. A cockfight, lasting somewhere between a few minutes and a half hour, usually results in the death of one or both of the birds. Cockfighting may have originated from religious ceremonies involving chickens. It is likely, however, that the use of chickens as food evolved earlier.

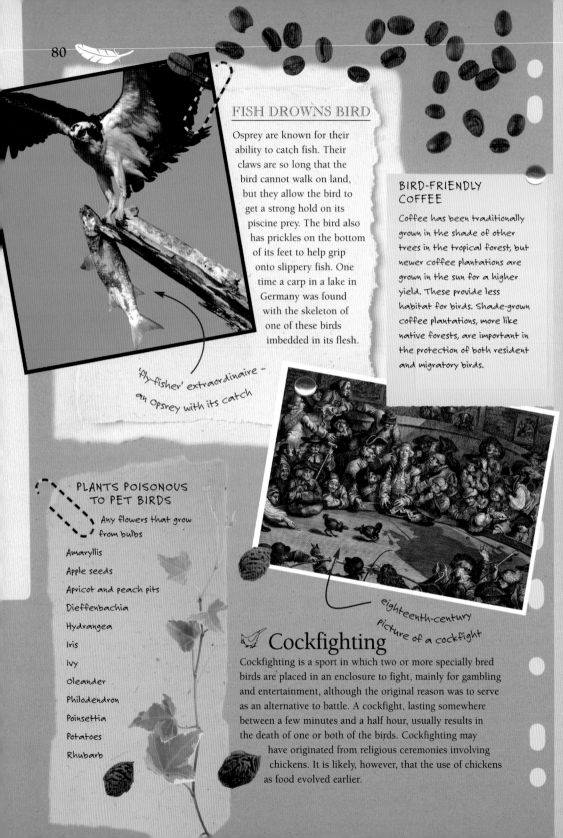

How Does a Woodpecker Peck Wood without Getting a Headache?

1 Woodpeckers have strong neck muscles, toes in an X arrangement (two each front and back) and a stiffened tail that allow them to climb vertically and hold on tight to the tree trunk while pecking.

2 Woodpeckers have a shock-absorbing mechanism in the skull, which allows the bones of the jaw to disconnect from the bones surrounding the brain at the moment of pecking.

3 In addition, their brain can withstand shocks almost ten times greater than humans, relative to their size.

4 The bill is made of bone with a keratin covering that continually grows, so it does not wear down completely.

5 The more they hammer for a living, the wider and stronger their ribs become.

headache? what headache?

DOCTOR BIRD

The Swallow-tailed Hummingbird of Jamaica is sometimes called the Doctor Bird because its black crest and long split tail resemble the top hat and tails doctors used to wear.

IT'S HARD WORK RAISING OFFSPRING

❖ The Great Tit may make nearly 1,000 trips per day to feed its young.

❖ The American Robin makes 400 trips a day.

❖ The Barn Swallow may make 1,200 visits a day.

❖ A pair of Puerto Rican Todies brought an estimated 280 prey items to their two chicks, while another pair delivered 420 items to a brood of three.

IS IT GOING TO RAIN?

❖ According to a city and county almanac of 1836, the arrival of the European Robin Red-breast is a sign of rain.

❖ Another sign of rain is the song of the Mistle Thrush, which sings louder before a storm and is sometimes called the Storm Fowl.

❖ The Swallow's behaviour of dipping its wings into the water is said to predict rain as well.

❖ According to some North American Indian beliefs, sparrows playing in the soil are a predictor of rain and their playing in water indicates that the weather will be dry.

a Robin Red-breast was once thought to be a harbinger of rain

a Harpy Eagle
in a display
of aggression

HEAVIEST PREY

❀ The Golden and Bald Eagles are often blamed for preying on young sheep or other animals. The Golden Eagle weighs up to 6 kg (13 lb) and the Bald Eagle up to 7 kg (15 lb). Although they can lift prey up to half their body weight, they mostly take prey far lighter than that.

❀ Golden Eagles typically take prey of about 1 kg (2–3 lb). They have preyed upon newborn sheep and even attacked mature animals, but their potential danger to domestic livestock is exaggerated.

❀ The heaviest prey item known to have been carried away by a bird was a 7 kg (15 ½ lb) monkey taken by a Harpy Eagle in Peru in 1990. The Harpy Eagle is one of the world's most powerful birds of prey, although the larger female weighs only 8.2 kg (18 lb).

all parrots have a characteristic curved beak – or should that be bill?

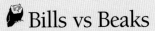

Bills vs Beaks

It used to be that parrots, hawks, eagles and vultures had beaks, curved-down structures for tearing fruit or flesh, and other birds had bills, more dainty pointed structures. However, the distinction has been lost and the terms are now used interchangeably.

MAGNETIC MISDIRECTION

In the 1970s, American biologist William Keeton placed non-magnetic brass bars on the backs of some homing pigeons and magnetic steel ones on others. Those with the magnetic bars attached had a harder time getting home than those with the brass bars, indicating that birds might be using geomagnetic lines of force to navigate, and the magnets interfered.

some birds might use geomagnetism to navigate

TERROR BIRD

Titanis walleri was the largest predatory bird ever, ranging up to 3 m (10 ft) in height. Related to modern-day cranes, it lived in the pampas of South America, chasing down prey at 70 kph (43 mph).

1901 drawing of a Terror Bird by Charles R Knight

PARROT GIFTS

In medieval Europe, exotic animals were status symbols and a mark of royalty and the wealthy. When Christopher Columbus returned to Spain from his voyage to the New World, he brought with him a pair of Cuban Amazon Parrots for Queen Isabella.

Christopher Columbus – explorer and exotic pet peddler

TEN THINGS TO KEEP YOUR PET BIRD HEALTHY

1. Provide a large, safe cage with appropriately placed perches.

2. Place the cage in a location away from draughts, other pets, houseplants and busy areas of the home.

3. Keep the cage clean; change water and food regularly.

4. Provide a healthy and varied diet.

5. Provide an interesting environment for the bird but do not allow unknown or possibly harmful objects to enter the cage.

6. Clip wings and claws whenever needed.

7. Close doors and windows when the bird is out of the cage.

8. Restrict and monitor the bird's activities when out of the cage.

9. When away from home, leave a radio or television on to prevent boredom.

10. Find a good veterinarian who has considerable bird experience.

I know you can still hear me without turning your head

Where Are Birds' Ears?

Birds' ears are located where ours are – on the sides of the head behind the eyes. Some appear to be merely holes in the skin and skull; others, such as owls', look similar to human ears. Owls, being more dependent on hearing than birds that are active in the daylight, have better hearing. One of the reasons is that the ears are asymmetrical (shaped differently) and one is positioned higher on the head than the other. As a result, each ear hears sounds differently and can pinpoint their location easily. Human ears, being symmetrical, cannot locate sounds if they are directly in front, above or behind our heads. This is why we have to cock our heads and move them around to locate some sounds (although owls do that as well).

a healthy pet Budgerigar

THE CINCINNATI ACCLIMATIZATION SOCIETY

Begun by a wealthy German named Andrew Erkenbrecher, who had emigrated to the US and made a fortune, the Cincinnati Acclimatization Society was dedicated to importing birds from Europe into Cincinnati because Erkenbrecher missed his homeland's avifauna. In the mid-1880s, Erkenbrecher arranged to import European birds to the US at a cost of $9,000 (£4,800) for 4,000 birds. Among these were the Song Thrush, the Corn Crake, the European Goldfinch, Nightingale and even House Sparrows and Common Starlings. Erkenbrecher and his associates acclimated the birds in an old mansion and finally released them without regard to the ecological havoc they could have produced; only the starling and sparrow survived.

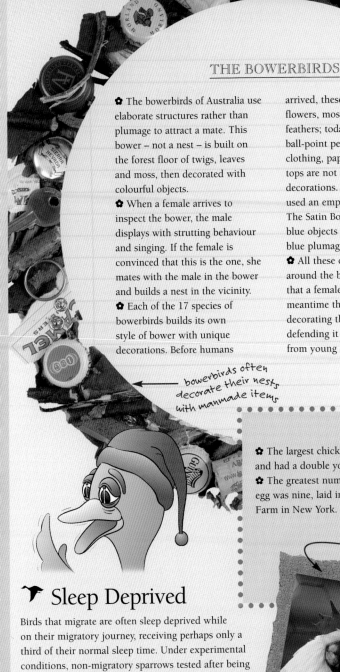

THE BOWERBIRDS

❀ The bowerbirds of Australia use elaborate structures rather than plumage to attract a mate. This bower – not a nest – is built on the forest floor of twigs, leaves and moss, then decorated with colourful objects.

❀ When a female arrives to inspect the bower, the male displays with strutting behaviour and singing. If the female is convinced that this is the one, she mates with the male in the bower and builds a nest in the vicinity.

❀ Each of the 17 species of bowerbirds builds its own style of bower with unique decorations. Before humans arrived, these objects were flowers, moss, berries and feathers; today the caps of ball-point pens, crockery, rubber, clothing, paper, pegs and bottle tops are not unusual bower decorations. One male even used an empty cigarette packet. The Satin Bowerbird prefers blue objects that match its shiny blue plumage.

❀ All these objects are scattered around the bower in the hope that a female comes by; in the meantime the male spends time decorating the bower and defending it from thievery, mostly from young males of the species.

← bowerbirds often decorate their nests with manmade items

WHAT A YOLK

❀ The largest chicken egg ever laid weighed 450 g (1 lb) and had a double yolk and double shell.

❀ The greatest number of yolks ever found in a chicken's egg was nine, laid in 1971 by a hen at Hainsworth Poultry Farm in New York.

hey there, did you know that a young hen like you can lay a yolkless egg?

🐦 Sleep Deprived

Birds that migrate are often sleep deprived while on their migratory journey, receiving perhaps only a third of their normal sleep time. Under experimental conditions, non-migratory sparrows tested after being sleep deprived showed a diminishing of brain function, but those in a migratory state showed little or no decrease in cognitive function. Apparently, the migratory state prepares birds both mentally and physically for the demanding journey.

US DEATH TOLL

❖ In the US, 60–80 million birds are killed by vehicles annually.

❖ Power lines cause the death of up to 174 million birds each year.

❖ Between 4 and 10 million birds are killed by lighted communication towers and guy wires each year. It has been estimated that the average cellular communications tower kills 2,500 birds per year. Birds flying in adverse weather conditions (fog, rain) at night are attracted to the towers' lights, which confuse the birds and cause them to collide with the tower.

❖ Pesticides kill approximately 60 million birds each year.

❖ Hunting (legal) accounts for the deaths of more than 100 million birds annually.

✒ Is the Ivory-billed Woodpecker Alive?

❧ The Ivory-billed Woodpecker may not be extinct. There have been a several claimed sightings in Florida and other US states over the past half century, even recently, but scientists do not agree as to whether the species still exists.

❧ North America's largest woodpecker had apparently become extinct in the United States after forest clearing destroyed millions of acres of virgin forest throughout the South between the 1880s and mid-1940s.

❧ This black-and-white bird lived in the old-growth forests of the southeastern United States and Cuba, eating primarily beetle larvae that it obtained by stripping the tree bark with its ivory-coloured bill. Because of its specialized feeding habits, the bird requires a large area of mature forests of dead standing trees.

❧ There are now efforts to save the Big Woods of Arkansas with a half million acres of bayous, wet forests and oxbow lakes. So far, the Nature Conservancy has purchased 18,000 acres (73 sq km) of this critical habitat. We still do not know if the bird exists.

GI JOE

❖ GI Joe is the most famous military pigeon of WWII, saving the lives of 1,000 British troops. A British brigade was supposed to attack the city of Colvi Vecchia, Italy, on the morning of 18 October 1943, after a bombing run by the US to soften the German defence. As it turned out, the Germans retreated before the bombing and the British entered the city early.

❖ Unfortunately, communication lines had failed and the bombing was still scheduled, so GI Joe was released with a message to cancel the bombing. The bird flew to the airbase just in time.

❖ General Mark Clark, Commander of the US Fifth Army, estimated that 'GI Joe saved the lives of at least 1,000 British allies.'

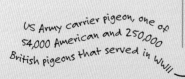

US Army carrier pigeon, one of 54,000 American and 250,000 British pigeons that served in WWII

Ivory-billed Woodpeckers, thought to be extinct, have been the subject of recent unconfirmed sightings

Do Birds Taste Good?

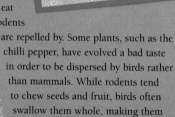

Cats have around 500 taste buds on their tongue, dogs 2,000, humans and pigs 15,000, and birds only a few dozen to a few hundred. Sometimes this is helpful because birds can eat distasteful fruits and nuts that rodents are repelled by. Some plants, such as the chilli pepper, have evolved a bad taste in order to be dispersed by birds rather than mammals. While rodents tend to chew seeds and fruit, birds often swallow them whole, making them much more likely to germinate later.

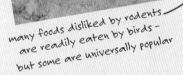

FLYCATCHER AIDS?

It was long thought that the rictal bristles (modified feathers) at the corners of the beak in flycatching birds serve as an aid in capturing prey. Research by the author of this book, using high-speed photography, demonstrated that this is not the case. The bristles are probably sensory, providing the bird with information on speed and orientation.

many foods disliked by rodents – are readily eaten by birds – but some are universally popular

BETTER TO NEST IN A HOLE?

On average, although there is a lot of variability, cavity nesters have a 66 per cent fledging rate (young birds hatching and leaving the nest). Birds that nest in the open have a fledging rate of about 50 per cent. Conclusion? Hole nesting is safer.

🦆 How Do Birds Mate?

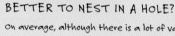

✿ There is a variety of mating circumstances, but in all cases a male mounts the female's back; the female lifts her cloaca (common urogenital opening) and moves it to the side to meet the descending male's cloaca, also moved to the side, and sperm is transferred.
✿ In ducks and a few other birds, the male has a penis that directs the sperm into the female's cloaca.
✿ In the case of swifts, mating occurs in midair; in the case of ducks, it happens on the water's surface, with the female partially submerged in the process.

♀ Pair of Wilson's Phalaropes mating

🦅 Linguistic Origins

the flamingo's name originates from the Latin for flame

Birds' names originate from many different languages. Here are a few examples:

🌼 **Greek**: The name pheasant comes from the Greek word *phasianos*, meaning of the Phasis River, which is now called the Rionos in the area of the Black Sea.

🌼 **Latin**: The plover's name ultimately derives from the Latin *pluvia*, meaning rain.

🌼 **French**: The linnet is named after its taste for *lin*, the Old French for flax seed.

🌼 **Gaelic**: The Capercaillie derives its name from the Gaelic *capull coille*, meaning horse of the woods.

🌼 **Latin**: The pink flamingo's name comes from the Latin *flamma*, meaning flame.

🌼 **Icelandic**: The Fulmar's name, from the Icelandic word *fúlmár*, meaning foul gull, derives from its nasty habit of spitting awful-smelling stomach oil at intruders.

🌼 **Latin**: Cormorant is derived from the Latin *corvus marinus*, meaning sea crow.

🌼 **Middle English**: Dotterel and coot both derive from Middle English words for old (and infirm) because these birds seemed rather slow and dull of wit.

🌼 **French**: Rail probably derives from the French dialect word *reille*, referring to the bird's cry. The phrase 'thin as a rail' does not refer to railroad tracks, but rather to these birds whose bodies are laterally flattened, giving them easier passage through the reeds and bulrushes they inhabit.

🌼 **Latin**: One of the most familiar birds, the canary, is named after its place of origin, the Canary Islands, but the islands themselves are named after dogs, from the Latin *canis*.

BIRDS HAVE ACCENTS

Bird populations have accents reflective of their geographical area. Individuals within a population also have voices that vary. If a population of birds lives near another population that has a similar accent, the birds of both populations have less variable voices than if they were isolated.

WHAT DO SEABIRDS DRINK?

Well, they drink saltwater. This, of course, poses a problem for them, as it would for us. Although their kidneys do extract some salt, their nasal glands eliminate most of the salt from the body. You might see seabirds sitting on the water sneezing; what they are actually doing is shaking their bills to rid them of the drops of salt that have accumulated there.

like all seabirds, gulls drink seawater

Barn Swallows build cup-shaped nests using mud

WANT A CHALLENGE?

Some bird nests are just flattish, cup-shaped nests built of thin twigs and grass. Look easy? Try to build one using these materials, first with your hands and then the way birds do it (no hands).

this nest is not as easy to build as it looks

WHITE AND BROWN EGGS

❖ White eggs are laid by chickens with white feathers and white ear lobes.

❖ Brown eggs are laid by chickens with red feathers and red ear lobes.

❖ There is no difference in taste or nutrition between white and brown eggs.

NEST BUILDING IN THE GENES

Nest building is genetic.

1 Every bird that builds a nest builds one characteristic of the species, with little variation.

2 Even birds raised in isolation build a nest typical of the species. However, some learning does occur, with older birds building better nests than younger, less experienced ones.

a Hyacinth Macaw – the biggest parrot in the world

Smallest and Largest Parrots

❖ The pygmy parrots of New Guinea and adjacent islands are about 7.7 cm (3 in) long and weigh about 65 g (2¼ oz).

❖ The Hyacinth Macaw of South America is the world's largest parrot, being about 100 cm (39 in) long and weighing 1.7 kg (60 oz) – 13 times longer and 26 times heavier than one of the New Guinea pygmy parrots.

FIRST BIRDKEEPERS

The first aviaries were built by the Romans in order to fatten birds for the dining table. The birds were fed figs that were pre-chewed by slaves.

Longest Bird Bill

❧ The longest bird bill, at up to 45 cm (18 in), belongs to the Australian Pelican.

❧ The Andean Sword-billed Hummingbird has the longest bill-to-body-length ratio. It is the only bird in the world with a bill longer than its body, an evolutionary response to the exceptionally long tubular flowers it feeds on.

the Sword-billed Hummingbird has an unusually long tongue, too

PIGEONS GO ON AND ON
The Rock Pigeon (feral pigeon of cities) may nest and raise young for 10 months of the year, having five or even six broods.

HEAVIEST FLYING BIRD: THE HEAVIEST BIRD THAT IS ABLE TO FLY IS THE GREAT BUSTARD AT 21 KG (46 LB).

BIRD POSTAGE STAMPS

❧ The first bird to be featured on a UK postage stamp was the Barn Swallow in 1957.

❧ First bird on a US stamp? Not surprisingly, the Bald Eagle, in the late 1800s.

❧ Over 25,000 stamps depicting birds have been issued across the world.

❧ Approximately 500 stamps from around the world depict the image of a chicken.

❧ The bird that occurs on more country stamps (43) than any other is the Hoopoe.

60c
BAHAMAS
BAHAMA MOCKINGBIRD

COLOMBIA
Onychorhyachus coronatus
$10.00
AEREO

Bahama Mockingbird and Colombian Royal Flycatcher stamps

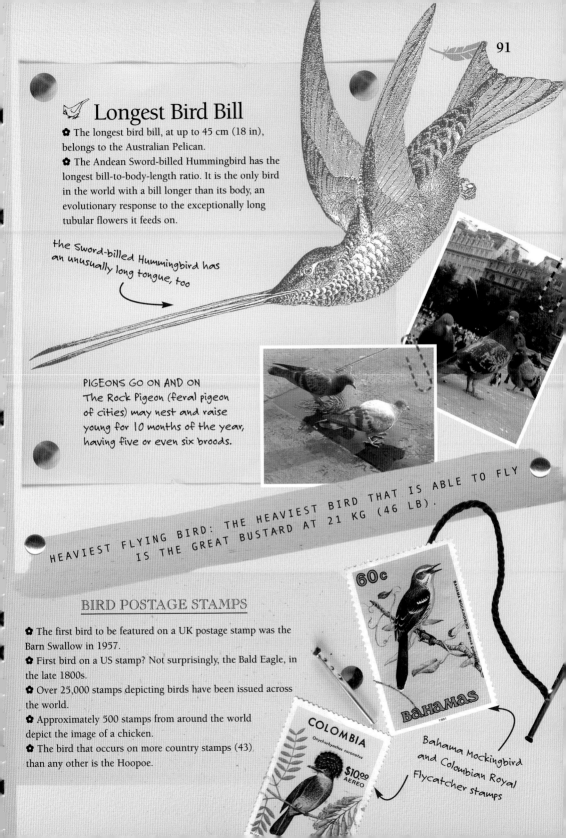

Clark's Nutcracker makes extremely varied sounds

Do Birds Sing Because They Are Happy?

It would be nice to believe that birds sing because spring has arrived and it is such a nice day. However, although no one can demonstrate what is in a bird's mind, it is unlikely that they sing simply for enjoyment.

1 Singing exposes birds to competitors and predators and takes time away from other essential activities, such as feeding and incubation.

2 It is a necessary behaviour to attract a mate and protect a territory.

3 There is an evolutionary trade-off between exposing oneself to predators and competitors and successfully breeding and raising young that makes singing worth the risk. A bird that sang for fun would simply risk being eaten for his frivolity.

BIRD SCARERS

❖ In medieval times in Britain, scarecrows were actually boys above the age of nine. Called bird scarers or bird shooers, they walked around wheat fields carrying bags of stones and chased off pest birds by waving their arms and throwing the stones.

❖ In the 1700s in Germany, Great Bustards were considered such crop pests that children were excused from school to help drive the birds from the fields.

❖ A Victorian bird scarer was a wooden device made of three pieces of wood that slapped together. Children stood in the fields and used it to make noise to stop birds from eating the newly planted seeds.

❖ Old men in some parts of India and the Middle East still sit in the fields and throw stones to scare birds.

scarecrows are still popular – try searching the internet for 'scarecrow festivals'

a Gentoo Penguin incubating an egg and displaying its brood patch

BROODING OVER THE YOUNG

Brooding is applying heat to eggs in order to incubate them and keep young birds warm. Feathers are great insulation, so brooding birds lose many of their central abdominal feathers; blood vessels in the bare skin swell and increase in number in order to transmit heat to the eggs and young. When not brooding, the adult bird can overlap the abdominal feathers on the side of this 'brood patch' to cover it.

a male Namaha Sandgrouse in the Kalahari Desert using its feathers like a sponge to carry water to its newly hatched chick

Snipe Hunt

Hunting snipe is a challenge because these birds inhabit marshes and have a quick, erratic flight. Although they are indeed hunted, a 'snipe hunt' has become a practical joke/fool's errand. The unsuspecting party, often as part of an initiation or some other ritual, is told to take a sack into the wetlands and capture snipe by hand after calling them. Of course, this is very unlikely.

WATERBOY

In the Kalahari Desert of southern Africa, the male sandgrouse soaks his abdominal feathers in a water hole and carries the water in his feathers back to the nest, where the young drink it. The feathers are capable of carrying 15–20 ml ($\frac{1}{2}$–$\frac{5}{8}$ oz) of water per 1 g ($\frac{1}{32}$ oz) dry weight of feather. A synthetic sponge can only hold 5 ml ($\frac{1}{4}$ oz) per 1 g ($\frac{1}{32}$ oz) dry weight.

SEABIRD HEAVEN: OVER 50 MILLION SEABIRDS NEST ON THE COASTS OF ALASKA – 87 PER CENT OF THE US SEABIRD POPULATION.

94

➤ Vulture Killer

In India, Pakistan and Nepal, vultures are dying of kidney failure due to a veterinary drug, diclofenac, that the vultures absorb when eating dead cattle that had been treated with the drug. Since the patent on the drug expired a few years ago, it became cheaper and more widely used. Luckily, conservationists have encouraged the use of a new non-lethal drug.

an Indian White-rumped Vulture eating dead cattle that could be infected

New Zealand stamp featuring a pair of monogamous Fiordland Crested Penguins

80c

NEW ZEALAND

ROMANTIC AROMA
The Crested Auklet, a seabird, produces a strong odour resembling the smell of tangerine that may be important in courtship. The birds of a pair nuzzle each other in the neck region where the aroma is produced.

EATEN TO EXTINCTION
The once abundant Wake Rail of Wake Island has the dubious distinction of having been eaten into oblivion by Japanese soldiers during World War II.

MONOGAMY

✿ Ninety per cent of bird species are monogamous, staying with one mate for the entire breeding season. The reason is obvious: a pair can raise young better than one individual can.

✿ However, it appears that most bird pairs do not mate for life, although there is evidence that some birds, including geese, eagles, cranes, ravens, wrentits, pigeons and albatrosses, maintain long-term pair bonds.

✿ Of these long-term pairs, 5–10 per cent separate each year to find new mates. In addition, if a partner dies, the remaining one will mate with another bird.

the Peregrine Falcon is not just the fastest bird; it is also the fastest creature when in its hunting dive

✝ Fastest Bird

Most ornithologists agree that the Peregrine Falcon deserves this designation (although no real scientific studies have confirmed this). Variously clocked at 300–400 kph (180–250 mph) in a dive while pursuing prey, they reach this speed by folding their wings against their body and dropping nearly straight down. In normal flapping flight, however, the Peregrine Falcon has accurately been measured flying at speeds of 36–70 kph (22–42 mph), with an average speed of 48.8 kph (29.3 mph).

NEED THAT BODY HEAT

During the first ten days of life, nestling songbirds do not show fear of an approaching predator. It is only from the sixth day on that a sense of fear begins to develop. The reason is that the hatchlings are not able to thermoregulate (maintain their body temperature) until after the fifth day. If they were to flee from a predator before being able to do so, they would surely die. After the sixth day, scattering from the nest might give them a chance.

DO BIRD FLOCKS HAVE LEADERS?

❖ High-speed photography has revealed that a flock of blackbirds or waders has no leader, at least for more than a few seconds at a time. The bird in front of a flying V or other formation will drop back and another will take its place at brief intervals.

❖ Any individual in the flock can initiate a turn and the rest of the flock will follow. This is why you might observe a flock flying back and forth – the lack of a leader produces the lack of a direction; but eventually the flock reaches a collective decision and goes in a particular direction.

❖ Why flock in the first place? Predators are less likely to attack a flock of birds than an individual, so a flock is protection against being eaten.

a Blue Tit attacking its own reflection in a car mirror

a 'glow-in-the-dark' Blue-and-yellow Macaw

Birds, Upon Reflection

❁ In the springtime, when hormones are flowing and male birds are trying to secure a piece of real estate in which to raise a family, they become territorial and aggressively chase away intruders, especially those of the same species.

❁ When the birds happen to come upon a reflection of themselves in a house window or car mirror, they may attack it vigorously. Pied Wagtails and Northern Cardinals seem especially prone to such behaviour. Useless as it is, they may fight this imaginary intruder for weeks.

❁ If you are disturbed by a bird participating in such behaviour, cover or block the source of the reflection. There is even a commercial windscreen for just such a problem.

CLAY LICKS

Parrots in South America frequent clay licks. These are usually walls of fine clay along a river, high in mineral content. Parrots, along with numerous butterflies, visit these licks and eat the clay, or at least chew on it. There is no definitive answer why, but it is thought that the minerals in the clay neutralize the toxins of the plants, seeds and nectar that the birds and butterflies eat.

PARROTS GLOW IN THE DARK

Although all birds have feather pigments that give them their colour, only parrots have a special yellow pigment that glows under ultraviolet light; the significance of this is unknown.

FOULING ONE'S NEST

While rapidly growing in the nest, young nestlings produce waste products. For precocial birds (those that leave the nest shortly after hatching), nest sanitation is not important. For others, some sort of sanitary measures are essential or the nest would become a haven for disease.

✿ Many songbird young produce a membranous faecal sac containing the waste products that a parent can pick up and dispose of.

✿ Some parent birds, such as the White-crowned Sparrow, actually swallow the faecal sacs to absorb some of the nutrients that the young were not able to process.

✿ Some young birds, such as hawks, herons and egrets, scoot to the rim of the nest and eject their waste over the side.

✿ Cormorants and shags simply ignore the whole business and end up with perhaps the dirtiest nests in the bird world.

Northern Shoveler

EYES ALL AROUND

When ducks rest on the ground in a flock, the birds on the perimeter of the flock sleep with one eye open – the eye away from the flock – in order to watch for predators, while birds in the centre tend to close both eyes for more restful sleep.

a clean and tidy Song Thrush nest

CITES

The Convention on International Trade in Endangered Species is the most important international law that regulates worldwide trade of many bird species and outlaws trade in the most endangered species.

WHY IS THE RAVEN BLACK?

Native American stories explain how the white raven turned black. In one version, the owl took the sun, moon and stars and hid them in his cave. The raven sneaked into the cave, stole these celestial bodies and hung them back in the sky, but while he was there, he also stole some embers from the owl's fire. As the raven flew with a beak full of embers, the smoke from the fire turned him black.

HERO BIRDS

After World War II, the military experimented with using birds to help locate pilots who ditched their planes in the ocean; birds could see downed pilots at far greater distances than humans.

MITEY INFESTATION

At least 2,500 species of feather mites are known to infect birds. Some dwell on the body of the bird and feed on blood, some eat the detritus that accumulates in the nest and some mites even feed on the bodies of blood-sucking mites. Whether mite infestations are harmful to developing chicks is up for debate.

Brood Size

Generally, the larger the brood size (number of young in the nest), the more trips the parents make to feed the young, but the number of feedings per nestling decreases at the same time. In addition, the bigger the brood, the lower the weight of each nestling and the lower the weight of the parents (due to the increased energy required to feed more young). Thus there is a limit to successful brood size.

a Great White Egret feeding its young

PIROUETTING PALM COCKATOO

The Palm Cockatoo displays to the female by pirouetting around the trunk of a dead tree with his wings outspread, his crest raised and beating on the trunk with a stick in his foot.

Palm Cockatoo

THE 24-HOUR EGG

After fertilization, the zygote (fertilized cell) moves down the oviduct (the passage from the ovary to the outside of the body) and accumulates all the nutrients, water, fibrous structure, shell and pigments that it needs before it is laid all in one day.

THE EXCEPTIONAL SHAG

❁ The cormorant or shag is an aquatic bird, both fresh and saltwater. In order to submerge effectively, cormorants do not oil their feathers and in fact, unlike most birds, have no oil glands. Hence they have to sit on a tree branch and spread their wings in order to dry out.

❁ Cormorants incubate their eggs by wrapping their webbed feet around them.

❁ King James I kept cormorants in an aviary on the River Thames in London and created a Keeper of the Royal Cormorants.

❁ Trained cormorants have traditionally been used in China and Japan for over 1,000 years to catch fish. With strings on their legs and a noose made of string or grass around their throat to prevent them from eating their catch, they are released from a boat and hauled back in with a fish in their gullet that is then massaged out by the human owner.

King James I – cormorant keeper

THE BARN OWL

❖ This light-coloured owl is found across most of the world, with the exception of Antarctica and the bulk of Asia, Canada and Alaska in North America, and the Sahara region of Africa.

❖ Its scientific name, *Tyto alba*, comes from the Greek *tuto*, meaning owl, and the Latin *alba*, referring to the colour white.

❖ The Barn Owl has also been called Barnyard Owl, Church Owl, Death Owl, Ghost Owl, Golden Owl, Monkey-faced Owl, Night Owl, Rat Owl, Screech Owl, Straw Owl and White Owl.

❖ The Barn Owl's eyesight is so acute that it can detect prey such as a mouse in a completely dark environment, in conjunction with its excellent hearing.

❖ In addition to seeing the mouse, the owl also reacts to the mouse's behaviour. As the owl swoops down for the kill, it aligns its talons with the long axis of the mouse, and if the mouse turns, the talons realign accordingly.

❖ The female Barn Owl is larger and darker than the male and has more spots. It seems to be that the more spots a female has, the fewer parasites she has, and so males are attracted to the most spotted females.

GREAT HORNED OWL ENEMIES

Great Horned Owls have no natural enemies, so aside from starvation, their major causes of mortality are human-related. Collisions with automobiles take a large toll, but an even greater danger is guns; in a study of ringed Great Horned Owls in the US, 46 per cent of their deaths were attributed to being shot.

Barn Owls are one of the most widely distributed of species that spread across the world naturally — that is, without human help.

SEEING IN THE DARK

An owl's eyesight in the dark is said to be 35 times better than a human's. This is equivalent to an owl seeing an object at its feet in near total darkness, with the only light being a match held 1.6 km (1 mile) away.

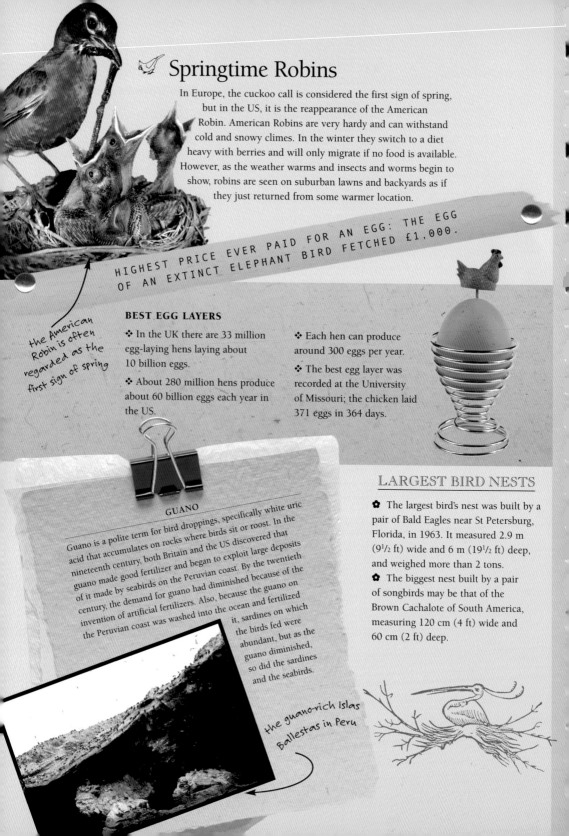

Springtime Robins

In Europe, the cuckoo call is considered the first sign of spring, but in the US, it is the reappearance of the American Robin. American Robins are very hardy and can withstand cold and snowy climes. In the winter they switch to a diet heavy with berries and will only migrate if no food is available. However, as the weather warms and insects and worms begin to show, robins are seen on suburban lawns and backyards as if they just returned from some warmer location.

HIGHEST PRICE EVER PAID FOR AN EGG: THE EGG OF AN EXTINCT ELEPHANT BIRD FETCHED £1,000.

the American Robin is often regarded as the first sign of spring

BEST EGG LAYERS

❖ In the UK there are 33 million egg-laying hens laying about 10 billion eggs.

❖ About 280 million hens produce about 60 billion eggs each year in the US.

❖ Each hen can produce around 300 eggs per year.

❖ The best egg layer was recorded at the University of Missouri; the chicken laid 371 eggs in 364 days.

GUANO

Guano is a polite term for bird droppings, specifically white uric acid that accumulates on rocks where birds sit or roost. In the nineteenth century, both Britain and the US discovered that guano made good fertilizer and began to exploit large deposits of it made by seabirds on the Peruvian coast. By the twentieth century, the demand for guano had diminished because of the invention of artificial fertilizers. Also, because the guano on the Peruvian coast was washed into the ocean and fertilized it, sardines on which the birds fed were abundant, but as the guano diminished, so did the sardines and the seabirds.

the guano-rich Islas Ballestas in Peru

LARGEST BIRD NESTS

✿ The largest bird's nest was built by a pair of Bald Eagles near St Petersburg, Florida, in 1963. It measured 2.9 m (9½ ft) wide and 6 m (19½ ft) deep, and weighed more than 2 tons.

✿ The biggest nest built by a pair of songbirds may be that of the Brown Cachalote of South America, measuring 120 cm (4 ft) wide and 60 cm (2 ft) deep.

WHITE DOVE RELEASE

To make sure that animals are not mistreated as a result of being released at a wedding or other function, groups such as the White Dove Release Association and International White Dove Society certify that their members release only white homing pigeons; these are white Rock Pigeons that have been trained to return home. Other doves (Turtle Dove, Ring-necked Dove) do not do well in this situation.

only white homing pigeons should be released at weddings

🕊 Birdy Proverbs

🕊 Birds of a feather flock together.

🕊 The early bird catches the worm.

🕊 A bird in the hand is worth two in the bush.

🕊 What's sauce for the goose is sauce for the gander.

🕊 Kill two birds with one stone.

🕊 Don't put all of your eggs in one basket.

🕊 Don't count your chickens before they are hatched.

🕊 One swallow does not make a summer.

🕊 A peacock has fair feathers, but foul feet.

I spy, with my little eye, something beginning with 'b' ... supper

SECRETARY BIRD

This bird gets its odd name from the 20 feathers sticking out from the back of its head that are reminiscent of the writing quills once used by secretaries. A native of Africa, it feeds largely on snakes. While attacking them with its powerful long legs and feet, the bird spreads out its wings in front of itself to avoid being bitten by any poisonous prey.

the proud peacock is used for adornment by artisans the world over

BIRDS AND CATS

Domestic cats kill 55 million birds each year in the UK and 100 million in the US. They kill four times as many rodents and are certainly not the only cause of bird population decline, but cats are definitely a threat.

Parrot Eating Habits

✿ The brush-tongued parrots (lorikeets) of Australia crush flowers with their beaks and lick up the nectar with their specialized fringed tongues.

✿ Hyacinth Macaws eat palm nuts, which are hard to husk. Some of these parrots have learned to drop the unhusked nuts where agoutis and other rodents live; the rodents husk the shell and leave the nut for the birds.

✿ Avocado is poisonous to parrots, especially African species.

✿ The Kea parrot of New Zealand has the unfortunate habit of chewing out the rubber seals around car windshields and wing mirrors.

some parrots eat nectar and nuts, but others have a taste for rubber

use a vinegar solution to clean birdbaths

THE BIRDS, BUT NOT THE BEES?

Birds can fly, but a myth persists that bumblebees cannot. Physical calculations of wing size and body weight indicate that bumblebees, and even some small birds, cannot fly. Actually, they can fly but they cannot glide – they flap their wings to produce lift.

HOW TO CLEAN A BIRDBATH

Wash the bath with water and a dilute solution of white vinegar. Water should be changed every few days.

DOVECOTES

Dovecotes are buildings made to attract and breed pigeons for food. Pigeons were once a major source of protein in Europe; at their height of importance, dovecotes may have numbered 25,000 in Britain alone. Dovecotes are still found in places such as Egypt today.

FOODS DANGEROUS TO PET BIRDS

Alcohol
Avocado
Caffeine
Chocolate
Fat
Onions
Rhubarb leaves
Salt

keep your pet bird healthy with safe, nutritious foods such as millet

traditional dovecote

OLD BIRDS

Some of the longest life spans of wild birds recorded during ringing studies are:

Little Corella	71 years
Royal Albatross	53 years
Laysan Albatross	50 years
Manx Shearwater	49 years
Black-footed Albatross	40 years
Great Frigatebird	38 years
Fairy Tern	35 years
Sooty Tern	35 years
Wandering Albatross	34 years
Arctic Tern	34 years
Red-tailed Tropicbird	32 years
Black-browed Albatross	32 years
Atlantic Puffin	31 years

The Holy Spirit

In Christianity the dove has been the most popular bird, honoured in the Old Testament for bringing Noah proof of the world's renewal after the flood. Even more important is the Genesis creation story that when 'the spirit of God moved upon the face of the waters', it had the form of a bird.

LONGER IS BETTER: INSECTIVOROUS BIRDS WITH LONG BILLS CAN CLOSE THEIR JAWS FASTER THAN BIRDS WITH SHORTER BILLS AND THUS CAN CATCH FASTER PREY.

woodpeckers carry fungal spores on their bills

EAR TUFTS

Many owls have ear tufts. These are most well-developed in nocturnal species of owls because they apparently help break up the silhouette of the cryptically coloured owl as it sits in a tree in the daytime.

many nocturnal owls have well-developed ear tufts

FUNGI HELPERS

Woodpeckers prefer to excavate nesting or roosting sites in dead trees. These dead trees are often softened by fungal decay. To return the favour, woodpeckers apparently carry fungal spores on their bills to other trees.

make a wish after eating your dinner

Making a Wish

✿ The wishbone, or furcula, is a Y-shaped bone formed by the fusion of the two clavicles, part of the shoulder skeleton. It helps to brace the wings against the sternum during flight.

✿ It is customary to take this bone out of a carved turkey or chicken and dry it. Two people then each hook a little finger around one fork of the Y and pull the bone apart while making a wish. The one who gets the longer piece will have his or her wish come true.

✿ An early name for the wishbone was the merrythought. The person who got the longer piece would marry first, producing merry thoughts.

✿ The custom of pulling the wishbone apart apparently derived from the Greylag Goose, whose wishbone was considered to be a strong indicator of forthcoming weather and supposedly even affected the direction of the First Crusade in 1096.

the Common Cactus Finch of the Galapagos Islands

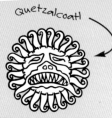

Quetzalcoatl

WHENCE THE QUETZAL

❖ The Resplendent Quetzal of Mexico and Central America, a spectacular member of the trogon family with iridescent tail feathers, appears on Guatemalan currency (the quetzal).

❖ The bird was a cultural force of both the Mayans and Aztecs, who made headdresses of their tails, and was the basis for the legendary Quetzalcoatl, a winged and feathered serpent who inspired poetry and works of art.

❖ The bright green bird has tail feathers over 60 cm (2 ft) long and looks like a shimmering serpent during flight. In order not to damage its tail feathers, the bird launches itself backwards off the branch before flying off.

TURKEY UMBRELLA

The Wild Turkey broods her chicks with her wings half open, like an umbrella, to protect them against the wind, rain and cold, and she will remain that way through the night.

DARWIN'S FINCHES

The 14 species of finches of the Galapagos Islands take considerable credit for making Darwin think about the process of evolution. Their basic form, with variations from island to island, indicated that local environmental conditions had something to do with the evolution of the physical form of the birds, particularly their bill, which varies from very slender to deep and heavy.

RICE AND BIRDS

In California and the Mississippi Valley where white and wild rice is grown, birds, particularly blackbirds of several species, can become pests. White rice sticks on the stalks but can be shaken off by birds landing on the stalks; wild rice is much more sensitive to being dislodged. Farmers use sound cannons to scare off the birds, workers to make noise or shoot at them, model airplanes, real airplanes and even distasteful chemicals. None of these methods is totally satisfactory.

birds like to eat rice and can become pests for farmers

ARRIVAL OF THE CHICKEN

The domestic chicken is a descendent of the Red Jungle Fowl of Asia and arose sometime between 3200 and 2000 BC. It is now probably the most common domestic bird.

CAMEL CONDOS

African sandgrouse nests are simply depressions in the ground – often in camel tracks – with little or no nesting material.

IT'S A MYTH: THE BELIEF THAT THE PARENT OF A YOUNG HAWK OR EAGLE THAT IS LEAVING THE NEST FOR THE FIRST TIME WILL CATCH THE FLEDGLING ON ITS BACK AND RETURN THE BIRD TO THE NEST IF IT CANNOT FLY HAS NO BASIS IN FACT.

the puffin sheds the coloured outer parts of its bill after mating season

 # The Puffin

✿ With their large, colourful beaks and clown-like looks, puffins are one of the most recognizable of seabirds.

✿ Except for eagles, puffins may be the most common subject of T-shirts, coffee cups, cards and souvenir plates.

✿ The name puffin originally meant fatling, referring to the young of the Manx Shearwater (a bird that is completely unrelated to puffins). Other names are clown of the ocean and sea parrot.

✿ The genus name *Fratercula*, meaning little brother or little friar, may have been chosen because puffins hold their feet together in flight as if they were praying or because of their black-and-white colour like a friar's robes.

✿ These seabirds winter on the ocean and dig burrows on land during the breeding season. They were sometimes considered a hybrid between a fish and a bird, which allowed Catholics to eat them on Friday instead of fish.

The Vampire Finch

As its name implies, the Vampire Finch, one of the Darwin's Finch group on Wenman Island in the Galapagos, feeds on blood. It generally feeds on Masked Boobies and Red-footed Boobies by pecking the skin forward of the tail until it bleeds. Why would such a habit evolve? Perhaps from an earlier behaviour of picking parasites off the boobies' skin, blood was drawn and the birds learned it was a source both of protein and liquid. The Vampire Finch is actually a subspecies of the Sharp-billed Ground Finch and is extremely rare.

strangely, boobies don't take evasive action – they allow Vampire Finches to feed on their blood

gulls are among the mere 300 species classified as seabirds

SEABIRDS

❯ Seabirds are birds that frequent open or coastal waters, such as pelicans, cormorants, boobies, albatrosses and petrels.

❯ A seabird makes its living from the sea, spending some or most of its time there, but returns to land to lay eggs.

❯ Of nearly 10,000 species of birds, fewer than 300 are classified as seabirds. Considering that the oceans cover about 70 per cent of the earth's surface, the percentage of seabirds is relatively small – about 3 per cent of the world's bird species.

❯ One of the major reasons there are so few seabird species is certainly that the ocean is a two-dimensional place for birds – they have to compete with other birds and sea life for the food on the surface or near the subsurface of the ocean.

HARPIES

These were beautiful winged women in Greek mythology who transformed into ugly women with sharp talons. The national bird of Panama, the Harpy Eagle, was named after them and was the model that artists used to create Fawkes the Phoenix for the movie Harry Potter and the Chamber of Secrets.

although sometimes thought to be Swiss, cuckoo clocks are actually German

CUCKOO CLOCK

The first cuckoo clock is thought to have been made around 1730 in Germany's Black Forest.

hey who are you calling a pest? oh, pesticide

NATURAL PESTICIDE

At one time German farmers used to trap European Robins in their houses to serve as insect catchers.

SWEETEST BIRD SONG CONTEST

In 2002, member organizations of BirdLife International competed via the internet to choose the best European bird song of the year. The public's top five were:

1 Golden Plover (a non-songbird)

2 Bluethroat

3 European Oystercatcher (also a non-songbird)

4 European Blackbird

5 Thrush Nightingale

list continues on page 108

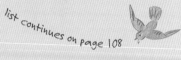

THE TWELVE DAYS OF CHRISTMAS

In this Christmas carol, the fourth day of Christmas was represented by four calling birds, referring to the four apostles, Matthew, Mark, Luke and John.

MOST WIDESPREAD BIRD: THIS IS PROBABLY THE HOUSE SPARROW, WHICH HAS SPREAD WITH THE HELP OF HUMANS.

Too Many Eggs in One Basket

❖ A few species of ducks that nest in tree cavities, such as the Wood Duck and Black-bellied Whistling Duck, engage in a strange behaviour known as dump nesting, in which a female duck will lay her eggs in the nest of another female, or even more than one.

❖ Sometimes a nest will be utilized by several females and the nest egg total may be in the dozens – even over a hundred in a few cases – although relatively few will hatch. If the female owner of the nest does not become frustrated and abandon it, she may lay hers on top of the other eggs and incubate them.

❖ Why do ducks do this? No one knows for sure. Speculations are that it might be due to a shortage of nest sites, inexperienced females not really knowing what to do or a deliberate attempt to have another female raise the young.

LONGEST INCUBATION: THE ROYAL ALBATROSS AT 81 DAYS. AFTER NEARLY THREE MONTHS IN THE EGG, THE CHICK THEN TAKES 3-6 DAYS TO HATCH AFTER MAKING A HOLE IN THE SHELL.

pet cockatiels live for 15-20 years, but wild ones only 12-15 years

VIKING NAVIGATORS

The Vikings took ravens with them when they sailed the North Atlantic and the North Sea. According to tradition, they would release a raven to determine their location and possible destination. If the raven flew back the way they had come and did not return, they knew they were still close to the place they had just left. If the raven came back to the ship, they knew there was no land in sight.

AVERAGE LIFE SPAN OF PET BIRDS

Cockatoos	65 years
Macaws	60 years
African Grey Parrots	50 years
Amazon Parrots	50 years
Conures	30 years
Doves	20 years
Pigeons	20 years
Lovebirds	20 years
Cockatiels	20 years
Budgerigars	20 years
Canaries	15 years
Finches	15 years

Which Binoculars Are Best for Birdwatching?

❖ Binoculars (two eyes) are like two telescopes mounted parallel to each other. At the front of each is a lens that gathers light and magnifies the image of the bird. The light goes through another lens in the eyepieces to your eye.

❖ Binoculars are described as being 7x35, 8x20, 10x50 or some similar figures. The first figure is the amount of magnification of the bird and the second is the diameter of the objective (biggest) lens in millimetres; larger diameters allow more light in and provide a wider view.

❖ So what size is best for seeing birds? Well, the greater the magnification and diameter, such as 10x50, the better the view of the bird, but the binoculars are too big and heavy for most people to carry around in the field. The smaller the numbers, such as 8x20, the lighter the binoculars, but the quality of viewing suffers proportionally as less light enters the lens. Most birdwatchers prefer 8x30 or 10x40 as a good all-round pair.

8x30 or 10x40 binoculars are good for birdwatching

sweetest bird song contest - list continued from page 107

Professional ornithologists thought differently, however, and rated birds, all songbirds, as follows:

1 Thrush Nightingale

2 Blackcap

3 Skylark

4 Marsh Warbler

5 Wren

list continues on page 109

Parrot Longevity

In general, larger parrots live longer than smaller parrots. Regardless of size, seed-eating (granivorous) parrots live longer than omnivorous or fruit-eating parrots. Rather than the diet, it may be due to the fact that granivorous parrots roost and travel in communal groups that assist in locating food and detecting predators.

sweetest bird song contest –
list continued from page 108

In the US, a more informal survey on the internet revealed these results:

1 Winter Wren

2 Veery

3 House Finch

4 Wood Thrush

5 Yellow-rumped Warbler

6 Baltimore Oriole

7 Cerulean Warbler

8 Red-shouldered Hawk

9 Northern Mockingbird

10 Field Sparrow/Prairie Warbler

big parrots usually live longer than small parrots

STATE BIRDS OF THE US

This listing uses the up-to-date American Ornithologists' Union names.

Alabama ....Yellowhammer
             aka Northern Flicker
Alaska ....Willow Ptarmigan
Arizona...................................Cactus Wren
Arkansas ....Northern Mockingbird
California ....California Quail
Colorado ....Lark Bunting
Connecticut ....American Robin
Delaware ....Blue Hen Chicken
Florida ....Northern Mockingbird
Georgia ....Brown Thrasher
Hawaii ....NeNe
Idaho ....Mountain Bluebird
Illinois........................Northern Cardinal
Indiana ....Northern Cardinal
Iowa ....American Goldfinch
Kansas ....Western Meadowlark
Kentucky....................Northern Cardinal
Louisiana...........................Brown Pelican
Maine ....Black-capped Chickadee
Maryland ....Baltimore Oriole
Massachusetts....Black-capped Chickadee
Michigan..........................American Robin
Minnesota...........................Common Loon
Mississippi............Northern Mockingbird
Missouri ....Eastern Bluebird
Montana ....Western Meadowlark
Nebraska ....Western Meadowlark
Nevada ....Mountain Bluebird

list continues on page 113

Poisonous Birds

❀ In 1992 it was confirmed that the feathers of the Pitohui genus of New Guinea contain a toxin. The skin of this bird can burn the mouth of whoever eats it in the same way a chilli pepper does.

❀ The same chemical is found in the poison-dart frogs of South America. It appears that neither the birds nor the frogs make the neurotoxin but probably acquire it in their diet.

❀ The distinctive red and black Hooded Pitohui's defence is so good that other birds, which do not possess the toxin, mimic the coloration to fool predators who know to avoid the toxic bird.

❀ The Blue-capped Ifrita, also found on New Guinea, possesses the toxin as well.

the Northern Cardinal is the official bird of seven US states

ARTIFICIAL LIGHT

A number of European birds are influenced by street lighting, and robins, song thrushes and blackbirds have all been noticed singing through the spring nights.

ROLLERS AND DIPPERS

❖ Rollers are named after their rocking-like motion in flight, when their body twists to the left and right.

❖ Dippers are named after their habit of bending the entire body up and down in a dipping motion.

the American Dipper is so-called because of its dipping movements

no, I'm not a eucalyptus tree, I'm a Tawny Frogmouth – can't you tell the difference?

Masters of Camouflage

Related to Oilbirds, Whip-Poor-Wills and nighthawks, the Tawny Frogmouth's excellent camouflage covering makes it look like dry leaves. When frightened, the bird freezes in position and, with its cryptic coloration, looks like broken branches. By remaining almost motionless with its camouflage, it can also entice prey to come close, at which point the bird snatches up the prey. With heart-shaped bills and large mouths, these birds can capture prey quickly and easily.

Crossed Bills

The crossbills are literally birds with crossed bills. The crossed mandibles are used to pry open the bracts of pinecones and extract the seeds. Because of their name and the colour of the Red Crossbill, legend has it that they used their crossed bills to remove the nails from Jesus' cross and they are thus found in medieval art.

Red Crossbill

city dwellers can attract birds with strings of popcorn

BIRDS IN THE CITY

Central Park in New York has over 100 bird species as visitors, so city dwellers can attract a variety of birds with a bit of effort.

1 Grow trees, shrubs and flowers in containers.

2 Provide bird feeders with seeds.

3 Hang bags of peanuts or strings of popcorn from the vegetation.

4 Try installing a birdhouse, such as for a kestrel or Blue Tit.

5 Provide fresh water.

6 Keep the area clean.

woodpeckers drill to find food, nest holes and roosting spots

BEING BIG HAS ADVANTAGES

Larger birds tend to have slower metabolisms than smaller birds, and some speculate that they live longer as a result. Seabirds and birds of prey may live 30 years or more.

WHY DO WOODPECKERS DRILL ON HOUSES?

1 In the spring they are seeking nest holes or insects and in the autumn a roosting site.

2 Soft wood is attractive to them, and it has been said that the vibration of electrical wires resembles the sounds of a termite colony.

3 Sometimes they are defending their territory or calling a mate by making drumming noises – in this case, they prefer metal or hard wood for louder noises.

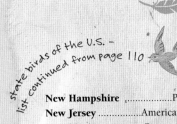

state birds of the U.S. – list continued from page 110

New Hampshire	Purple Finch
New Jersey	American Goldfinch
New Mexico	Greater Roadrunner
New York	Eastern Bluebird
North Carolina	Northern Cardinal
North Dakota	Western Meadowlark
Ohio	Northern Cardinal
Oklahoma	Scissor-tailed Flycatcher
Oregon	Western Meadowlark
Pennsylvania	Ruffed Grouse
Rhode Island	Rhode Island Red
South Carolina	Carolina Wren
South Dakota	Ring-necked Pheasant
Tennessee	Northern Mockingbird
Texas	Northern Mockingbird
Utah	California Gull
Vermont	Hermit Thrush
Virginia	Northern Cardinal
Washington	American Goldfinch
West Virginia	Northern Cardinal
Wisconsin	American Robin
Wyoming	Western Meadowlark

Greek playwright Aristophanes included lots of birds in his work

ARISTOPHANES' THE BIRDS

Greek dramatist Aristophanes made considerable use of birds – 80 species, in fact – and wrote a comic play, *The Birds*, in 414 BC. He was one of the first authors to make extensive use of birds in literature.

FASTEST AND SLOWEST WING BEATS

Many hummingbirds have very fast wing beats, from 50 to 80 per second, but the record might be held by the Horned Sungem of South America at 90 beats per second.

The slowest wing beats, at one beat per second on average while flying, are found among vultures.

hummingbirds' wings beat very quickly

owls have excellent low-light vision

LOW-LIGHT VISION

❖ The retina (the layer of photosensitive cells at the back of the eye) has cells called rods (for black-and-white vision) and cones (for colour). Humans and birds both rely on rod cells to see in low light conditions.

❖ The human eye has 200,000 rod cells per square millimetre, while owls may have 1,000,000 rods per square millimetre.

Bearded Greenbuls use ferns to build their nests

↑ Lead Poisoning

❖ Experimental feeding of Mallards by lead shot (from shotguns) resulted in a 90 per cent mortality rate, while birds fed with steel shot were not affected.

❖ Mute Swans in the UK were killed after swallowing lead weights lost or discarded by anglers. Today, lead-free weights are used.

❖ Great Northern Divers (aka Common Loons) suffer a significant number of deaths (10–50 per cent) by consuming lead fishing weights.

LEAFY CAMOUFLAGE

❖ Bearded Greenbuls of Africa incorporate a living fern plant into their nests.

❖ Of the many Australian bird species that nest in trees, 66 per cent nest in mistletoe. The plant apparently provides additional structure and camouflage for the nest.

❖ Tailorbirds of Asia use their sharp beaks to make holes along the edges of leaves. They then sew the edges of the leaves together with silk, wool, hair and fibre to make a cradle in which to build a grass nest.

pelicans rapidly vibrate their upper throat skin to help them cool down

GULAR FLUTTERING

✿ Gular fluttering is an energy-efficient method used by various birds to dissipate body heat in hot environments. Birds can keep cool by panting, but panting requires greater energy relative to the amount of heat lost.

✿ Gular fluttering involves vibrating and flapping of the upper throat skin. A plexus of veins in the throat area acts as a heat exchanger, with water and heat being lost from the skin membranes of the throat.

✿ This behaviour is commonly seen in pigeons, pelicans, chickens, doves, quail, nighthawks, cormorants, owls and the roadrunner.

chickens indulge in gular fluttering, too

NEST RELIEF CEREMONIES

In many species of birds, the male and female engage in some sort of greeting ceremony before exchanging duties on the nest. For example, an avocet incubating eggs will stand up and bow to its approaching mate, who returns the bow. Then they engage in some straw- or stick-throwing behaviour before they switch roles and the incubating one goes off to search for food.

a seagull gliding on the wind

Doesn't Gliding Get Tiring?

When a bird glides, it is holding out its wings for long periods of time. One mechanism that helps to avoid fatigue is a tendon that runs along the back of the ulna (a wing bone) and attaches to the secondary feathers. These are the feathers that produce lift and the tendon assures that all the feathers are spread at the proper distance at all times.

LAND OF BIRDS

The original set of animals of New Zealand featured no mammals, so the islands were once called the Land of Birds.

BIG EGG: It takes two hours to hard-boil an ostrich egg. One ostrich egg is equivalent to 24 chicken eggs, and it takes only one ostrich egg to fill up a frying pan.

Australian Gannet (3D) and Kokako ($1) featured on New Zealand stamps

1858 · HAWKES BAY CENTENNIAL · 1958 3D
CAPE KIDNAPPERS NEW ZEALAND

kokako $1
NEW ZEALAND

a killdeer's speckled eggs are well camouflaged against the surrounding stones

VULTURES AND STORKS

Old World (Asia, Europe, Africa) vultures are related to hawks and eagles; New World (North and South America) vultures are more closely related to storks.

NON-MIGRATORY BIRDS HAVE MORE KIDS

Large – over 2 kg (4.4 lb) – non-migratory birds have larger clutches and longer fledgling times than large migratory species. Apparently, the need to begin migration is more important than the number of eggs laid or the benefit of a full fledgling period.

ostriches – which don't fly anywhere – lay large communal clutches

IMPROVING AIRPLANES

Researchers at Oxford University mounted a tiny camera on the back of an eagle to monitor its flight movements, and scientists at the University of Florida have built airplanes modelled on gulls' wing shapes. They hope these experiments will lead to better airplane design.

IT'S A TRICK!

❀ Lapwings and Killdeer build a simple nest, often just a depression in the ground in the open, in marshes or in grasslands. The eggs are well camouflaged with mottled patterns that mimic the gravelly ground; when the chicks hatch, the parents carry off the shells because the open eggshell with its white interior spoils the camouflage.

❀ Despite the camouflage and precautions, the location of the nest makes the eggs vulnerable to foxes and other hungry creatures. To protect her eggs when a predator approaches, the incubating female flees the nest, dragging a wing along the ground, feigning injury, followed by the hungry but duped predator. At some point she flies off. This behaviour is common among waders as well as a few other types of ground-dwelling birds.

❀ Some birds, such as sandpipers and sparrows, run away from their nests with both wings trailing behind, looking like a mouse. The predator, once again tempted by a bigger prize, gets nothing after the bird takes flight.

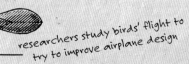

researchers study birds' flight to try to improve airplane design

Hiding in a Hole

The 54 species of hornbills are found in Asia, Africa and Australasia and get their name from a large growth on the upper mandible of many species. The female hornbill lays eggs in a hollow tree, and the hole of the nesting cavity is closed in by the male with clay except for a small hole. This affords the female protection against predators. The male feeds his mate through the small hole and may visit the nest 20 times each hour. As the young grow, the female breaks out of the nest and the youngsters close the opening through which the mother has escaped. Once the young grow large, they break free from the nest as well.

Great Hornbills

since having the kids, I just don't seem to get out much

LEKS

A lek is a communal display area in which the males of polygynous species (males mating with more than one female) strut, call, sing and display to admiring females who only visit the lek to find a male and mate. In lek species, such as manakins, grouse, prairie chickens and Lesser Birds of Paradise, the male takes no part in caring for the eggs or young.

I wonder who the blue-and-grey one's dad is...

✌ What Is a Species?

A species is defined as a group of individuals capable of interbreeding with each other but not with another group defined as another species. Most birds abide by the definition, but there are exceptions, such as a Common Buzzard mating with a Goshawk, and a Pintail duck hybridizing with a Mallard. However, the young from these mixed-species pairings are usually infertile.

humans have introduced bird species to new habitats around the world – some fit in more successfully than others

SPECIES INTRODUCTIONS

🖋 *Humans have transported around 5 per cent of bird species to new environments.*

🖋 *This has involved about 2,000 attempts to introduce 400 species to new habitats across the world.*

🖋 *Of those birds that were introduced, two-thirds belong to only six families: waterfowl, pheasants and allies, pigeons, parrots, sparrows and finches.*

many gulls have a red spot on their beaks

BEGGING FOR FOOD

Dutch ethologist Niko Tinbergen, who shared a Nobel Prize in 1973 with Austrian ethologists Konrad Lorenz and Karl von Frisch for their work in animal behaviour, discovered that the red spot on the yellow bill of many gulls functions to elicit a begging response from young chicks. When the chicks see the spot, they peck at it; when the parent senses the pecking, it regurgitates food.

THE CANARY

The song of canaries
Never varies,
And when they're moulting
They're pretty revolting.
– Ogden Nash

THE FAIRY TERN

🖊 The only all-white tern, with a blue bill, Fairy Terns breed in trees, but do not build a nest. The female finds a broken stub or fork of a limb or branch where she deposits a single egg.

🖊 Here she incubates the egg for three weeks, after which a fluffy chick is hatched. Fed fish by both parents, the chick is able to maintain its perch with its overly large feet.

🖊 Fairy Terns have large eyes and it is thought that this is an adaptation for hunting for fish in the dark.

Fairy Terns lay their eggs on branches, so their chicks have big feet to hold onto their perches

🐦 Why Do Some Birds Not Fly?

In the evolutionary history of birds, the ability to fly emerged and many bird species became quite adept at it. Only later did some birds lose the capacity for flight. Why?

1 Flight is energetically expensive and requires special adaptations. If a bird does not need to fly, these adaptations will be lost.

2 Since the main reason that flight was so useful in the first place was to escape predators, birds that live in places with few or no predators lost the ability to fly. Many flightless birds evolved on islands with few or no land predators: the kiwis of New Zealand, the Galapagos Cormorant and the penguins of Antarctica.

3 Another way to avoid predators is to be big and strong and have the ability to run fast, so again flight is not necessary. Fitting the bill are the rheas of South America, the ostrich of Africa, the extinct moas of New Zealand and the emus of Australia.

the ostrich is big enough to deter many predators, and if that doesn't work, it can run away

BEST-KNOWN MIGRATION SPOT IN NORTH AMERICA

Point Pelee in southern Ontario, Canada, is a famous location at which to watch migrating birds. More than 360 species of birds pass through Point Pelee in the autumn and spring, and more than 100 species can be spotted in a day. The southward migration is spread over a longer period and is more casual than the relatively frantic northward migration.

Point Pelee National Park is also known as the Wood Warbler capital of North America, with 42 of North America's 55 species migrating through this area.

Canadian stamp featuring a Canada Goose

GREAT HARVEST

In the late nineteenth century in the US, hunters in the Midwest shipped as many as 500,000 waterfowl, songbirds and waders at a time to markets in Chicago, St Louis and elsewhere.

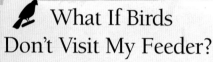

What If Birds Don't Visit My Feeder?

It often takes a while, sometimes months, before a bird feeder becomes popular. Assuming that the bird feeder is in a good place and that a sufficient variety of quality seeds are offered, the reason may simply have to do with the time of year. Autumn, winter and early spring are the times when seed-eating birds are searching out food. The rest of the year, natural foods are available in the wild. In addition, bird parents feed their young on high-protein foods such as insects and worms rather than seeds. Put out your feeder for the first time in midsummer and visitors will be scarce. As autumn approaches, birds will flock to your feeder.

ISLAND OWL EXTINCTION

Every owl that has gone extinct in the last 300 years lived on an island.

RED EYE

Nocturnal birds have a reflective layer behind the retina of their eyes that serves to reflect light back through the retina and allows birds such as nighthawks and owls to see better in the dark. This layer is also what causes the birds' eyes to glow red when a light is shone on them.

the popularity of bird feeders is seasonal

RUBBERY EGGS

Eggs are strong because they contain a shell of calcium. The calcium is laid down over a matrix of protein fibres. If you put a raw chicken egg in a glass of vinegar, a weak acid, in a day or two the calcium will dissolve and you will be able to see the protein matrix. You can even handle the egg, now rubbery, without harm to its innards.

calcium makes eggshells strong

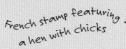

French stamp featuring a hen with chicks

La poule

RF DRUCKION

0,50 €

INFANTICIDE

In situations where the food supply is limited, parent birds may ignore or even kill the smallest or weakest of their clutch in order to provide food for the others.

eiderdown from far northern climes is prized throughout the world; here, a man is making eiderdown quilts in Jerusalem in 1953

🐦 Icelandic Eiderdown

🌸 When Iceland was settled by Norwegians in the ninth century, they took with them the tradition of eiderdown. In 1651, King Christian IV of Norway decreed protection of eider nesting colonies in northern Iceland because he was so impressed with the birdlife there.

🌸 The female eider duck plucks down from her breast to line the nest and cover the eggs. Once the young hatch and the nest is abandoned, the eiderdown is gathered. The birds are not harmed, and are actually attracted to these safe areas by the farmers, who supply food and protect birds from poachers. This relationship

between wild eider duck and farmer has existed for generations.
🌸 Today, the Icelanders are almost the only people who continue to produce eiderdown. From the feathers of nests – not plucked – four tons of eiderdown per year are produced, three of which are from Iceland, the rest from Scandinavia.

ZUGUNRUHE

The urge to migrate,
known as zugunruhe,
expresses itself in birds by anxious behaviour and eating a
lot to put on fat. This behaviour was first noticed by cage
bird fanciers among wild birds restricted to cages, and has
since been used in a number of studies of bird migration
and the effect of the environment on bird hormones.

Hawaii's state symbol, the NeNe, is the world's rarest goose

Canadians Move to Hawaii

The state bird of Hawaii is the NeNe goose, which was once thought to be a sister species (derived from the same ancestor) of the Canada Goose. Recent research has revealed that the NeNe is actually a descendent of the Canada Goose. In fact, the NeNe is more closely related to some subspecies of Canada Goose than the subspecies are to each other. So, sometime about 500,000 years ago, some Canada Geese made it to Hawaii, where they eventually gave rise to the NeNe.

John F Kennedy had a canary and a couple of parakeets

PRESIDENTIAL PETS

Many US presidents have kept birds as pets. Here are some of them:

JOHN F KENNEDY – Robin (canary); Bluebell and Marybelle (parakeets)

CALVIN COOLIDGE – Nip and Tuck (canaries); Snowflake (white canary); Old Bill (thrush); Enoch (goose)

MRS WARREN HARDING – Canaries

THEODORE ROOSEVELT – Eli Yale (macaw); a one-legged rooster

MRS GROVER CLEVELAND – Canaries and mockingbirds

RUTHERFORD HAYES – Mockingbird

ULYSSES S GRANT – Parrot and gamecocks

ZACHARY TAYLOR – Johnny Ty (canary)

MRS JAMES MADISON (Dolly) – Green parrot

THOMAS JEFFERSON – Mockingbird

MRS GEORGE WASHINGTON – Parrot

LONGEST WINGSPAN

✿ The longest measured wingspan on any living bird is that of the Wandering Albatross at 3.6 m (141 in) from wing tip to wing tip – wider than the smallest airplane, which has a wingspan of only 2.18 m (86 in).

✿ The Teratorn of South America, which lived 6–8 million years ago, had a wingspan of about 7.5 m (25 ft).

Wandering Albatross

Largest and Smallest Eggs

✿ The largest egg of any living bird is that of the ostrich,
at approximately 12.5–15 cm (5–6 in) in diameter,
15–18 cm (6–7 in) in length and with a 3 mm (⅛ in)
thick shell.

✿ The largest egg ever laid by a bird was that of the
Elephant Bird of Madagascar. Extinct since about 1700,
it is the largest bird known, with an egg 15 times larger
than an ostrich egg. An omelette made from an Elephant
Bird's egg would serve 75 people.

✿ The smallest bird egg is certainly that of a
hummingbird. The smallest hummingbird egg is
the 0.2 g egg of the Bee Hummingbird of Cuba.
The Vervain Hummingbird of the Caribbean comes
in second with an egg that weighs 0.375 g.

the drumming of a woodpecker is a form of communication

NON-VERBAL COMMUNICATION

❖ The flightless and nocturnal
kiwis of New Zealand stomp
their feet when disturbed.

❖ Storks clap their bills.

❖ Roadrunners vibrate
their mandibles.

❖ Woodpeckers drum on
trees or other objects.

❖ Some snipe vibrate their tail
feathers in flight to prodcue a
'drummy' sound.

❖ The honeycreepers of Hawaii
have a noisy flight.

❖ Some nighthawks and
hummingbirds fly to considerable
heights, dive and spread their wings
to make a booming sound. Because
of this sound, nighthawks were
once called bullbats.

the eggs of an Elephant Bird, ostrich and hummingbird – guess which is which

eggs contain built-in shock absorbers, such as egg white, to protect the embryo

Shock Absorbers

🖋 As the egg develops and descends through the oviduct, the albumen (egg white), which is mostly protein, serves initially as a shock absorber for the egg and later for tissue growth in the developing embryo.

🖋 The stringy whitish mass one observes in a cracked-open egg is called the chalaza, which also serves as a shock absorber for the embryo of the egg.

🦆 Lily Trotter

The jacanas of Central and South America, Asia and Africa have long legs and extremely long toes and claws in order to walk across lily pads and other floating vegetation on which they nest. If the nest threatens to sink, the male will pick up the eggs under his wings and walk with them to another site. Once the young hatch, the male may transport them under his wings as well, with their gangly legs dragging.

SMALLEST AND LARGEST KINGFISHERS

❀ The African Dwarf Kingfisher weighs a mere 9–12 g ($^{5}/_{16}$–$^{7}/_{16}$ oz).

❀ The Australian Laughing Kookaburra may reach 490 g ($17^{1}/_{4}$ oz).

Australian Laughing Kookaburra

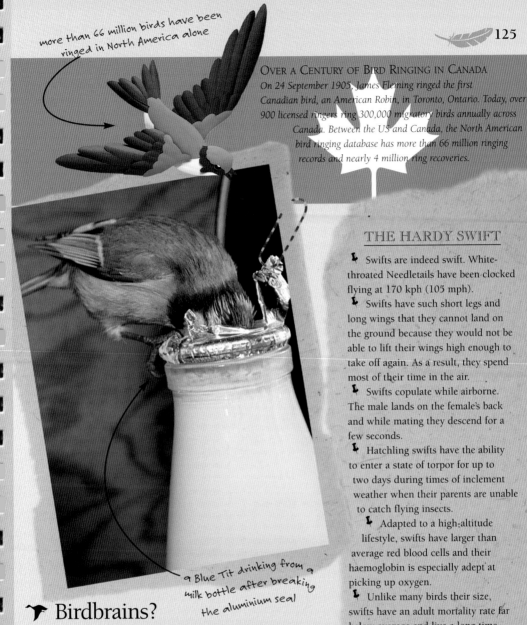

more than 66 million birds have been
ringed in North America alone

OVER A CENTURY OF BIRD RINGING IN CANADA

On 24 September 1905, James Fleming ringed the first
Canadian bird, an American Robin, in Toronto, Ontario. Today, over
900 licensed ringers ring 300,000 migratory birds annually across
Canada. Between the US and Canada, the North American
bird ringing database has more than 66 million ringing
records and nearly 4 million ring recoveries.

*a Blue Tit drinking from a
milk bottle after breaking
the aluminium seal*

THE HARDY SWIFT

❧ Swifts are indeed swift. White-throated Needletails have been clocked flying at 170 kph (105 mph).

❧ Swifts have such short legs and long wings that they cannot land on the ground because they would not be able to lift their wings high enough to take off again. As a result, they spend most of their time in the air.

❧ Swifts copulate while airborne. The male lands on the female's back and while mating they descend for a few seconds.

❧ Hatchling swifts have the ability to enter a state of torpor for up to two days during times of inclement weather when their parents are unable to catch flying insects.

❧ Adapted to a high-altitude lifestyle, swifts have larger than average red blood cells and their haemoglobin is especially adept at picking up oxygen.

❧ Unlike many birds their size, swifts have an adult mortality rate far below average and live a long time – more than 20 years in many cases. Given their propensity to flight, they will have flown perhaps 6 million km (4 million miles) in that time.

➤ Birdbrains?

Although birds do more by instinct than learning, they certainly are capable of learning, as amply demonstrated by the Blue Tit in England. In the early twentieth century, deliveries of milk bottles to the door were commonplace. These milk bottles had only a paper top, so birds had easy access to the cream that settled in the top of the bottle by pecking through the paper. This discovery, probably made by one or a few birds, spread throughout the entire tit population in a few years. Then, before WWII, dairy distributors placed aluminium seals on their bottles to foil the birds. By the early 1950s, however, the entire Blue Tit population had learned how to pierce the aluminium seals.

The Great Crested Grebe is an excellent swimmer and diver

STICK TO THE WATER

Grebes dive to escape danger rather than fly. Their legs are set far back on their body, making walking more difficult, so they rarely set foot on dry land. Their lobed feet are more than sufficient transportation in the water.

In the Clutches of Nature

✿ The size of a clutch (group of eggs) depends on a lot of factors: bird species, climate, whether or not both parents incubate and care for young, whether the young are altricial (helpless) or precocial (advanced) when hatched, size of the egg and so on.

✿ In general, clutch sizes are larger farther away from the equator (where the nesting season is shorter than nearer the equator), and larger in domed or hole nests where climate and predators are less of a factor than for open-cup nests.

✿ Birds will have as many young as they can possibly raise in their particular environment.

✿ Ducks, larger birds with precocial young that can leave the nest and feed independently right after hatching, can have more young, even though only the mother provides parental care.

✿ Penguins in the Antarctic face a very harsh environment. Even with both parents incubating and providing food, only one or two eggs are laid.

FLYING BACKWARDS

Hummingbirds commonly fly backwards. The Red-tailed Tropicbird (a seabird) has been known to do so also during its courtship behaviour.

hummingbird

Black-bellied Whistling Ducks

1, 2, 3, 4, 5...oh, not again – where's the other one gone?

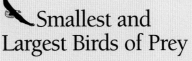

Smallest and Largest Birds of Prey

🪶 The smallest is the White-fronted or Bornean Falconet of northwestern Borneo at 14–15 cm (5½–6 in) long, including a 5 cm (2 in) tail, and a weight of 37 g (1¼ oz).

🪶 The largest is the Andean Condor of western South America at a height of 3.6 m (4 ft), with a wingspan of 3 m (10 ft) and a weight of 9–13.6 kg (20–30 lb).

the Andean Condor is the largest bird of prey

HEART AND LUNG COORDINATION: APPROXIMATELY NINE TIMES FOR EVERY A BIRD'S HEART BEATS BREATH.

THE DANCE OF THE CAPERCAILLIE

The Capercaillie is the largest grouse in the world. Male birds have a complex display to attract females in a communal affair at a traditional site known as a lek. The display song involves tapping and gurgling followed by a noise similar to a cork being pulled out of a bottle, while the male holds his tail vertical and fanned out with his beak pointing up. He struts forward and often does a flutter-jump, leaping rapidly with noisily flapping wings.

the Capercaillie's impression of a cork being pulled out of a bottle impresses females

WHY DO BIRDS FLY?

1 Initially, birds evolved the power of flight to escape predators.

2 Flight then became extremely useful in the search for food.

3 It is also used to find nest sites.

4 Birds fly to look for appropriate habitats.

5 Birds fly to find the best climate.

Danish stamp featuring the Skylark

SANGLÆRKE
ALAUDA ARVENSIS
DANMARK 2.80

FATHER OF AMERICAN ORNITHOLOGY

Alexander Wilson was born in Scotland in 1766. Apprenticed as a weaver, he later became a peddler and poet. In 1794 he moved to the United States where he was a school teacher, but his strong desire to learn about birds and his powers of observation made him an expert on birds. He ultimately published American Ornithology *between 1808 and 1813, one of the most elaborate books of the time.*

Alexander Wilson

she started teaching me to talk when she was just a girl, you know

🐦 Six Rules for Teaching Your Parrot to Talk

1 Make sure your bird is healthy.

2 Start with short, frequent sessions.

3 Use small words first, such as *hi*, *hello*, and *birdie*.

4 Reward your bird with praise when he or she responds.

5 Don't add more words until the bird learns the first one.

6 Be positive – some birds learn more slowly than others.

EIGHT RULES OF BIRD FEEDING

1 Offer food in several places and change location often so that the feeding sites do not become heavily contaminated. Avoid feeding large numbers of birds at the same feeder for a long time.

2 Keep the ground beneath feeders clean or move the feeders regularly.

3 Keep surfaces on which birds feed clean.

4 After cleaning, feeders can be disinfected by washing or soaking for a few minutes in a 5 per cent sodium hypochlorite (bleach) solution. Rinse all surfaces thoroughly.

5 Any water provided should be clean and containers regularly disinfected.

6 Use only fresh foods; mouldy foods attract bacteria.

7 Use rubber gloves when cleaning feeders and baths.

8 Watch for signs of illness in birds at feeding sites and notify the proper authorities if you see such signs. Green Finches are particularly susceptible to outbreaks of salmonella.

a Lesser Adjutant Stork perched in a tree

ADJUTANT STORKS

The Lesser Adjutant Stork has a featherless head and feeds in muddy water; often the head turns green because algae grow on the bird's scalp. British troops in India named these storks because the birds' pompous way of striding reminded them of their senior officers, called adjutants.

clean, well-stocked feeders will help keep garden birds healthy

BIRD POPULATION TRENDS

Under stable conditions, bird populations fluctuate each year. In most cases the populations may only vary 10–20 per cent each year, but unusual increases or decreases in food sources or drastic changes in weather can cause more severe population declines or moderate increases.

European Robin

IT'S A DIFFICULT LIFE: ONLY ABOUT ONE IN FOUR EUROPEAN ROBINS SURVIVES TO MATURITY.

THE LAMMERGEIER

Named from the Old German meaning Lamb Vulture, this bird is one of the largest of raptors. Found in parts of Africa, the Middle East and Asia, it eats a variety of small birds and mammals but most of its diet consists of the bone marrow of large mammals like the horse. It will take an arm or rib from a carcass, fly high over a rock and let it drop, splintering the bone. The bird picks up the shards and swallows them. The strong stomach acids do the rest.

horse carcass provides the Lammergeier with plenty to chew on

🐦 How Do Birds Eat Without Teeth?

❀ In the course of evolution, birds lost their heavy teeth as a weight-loss adaptation for flight. Instead, the much lighter beaks became adapted for various other ways of catching or eating food items by being sharp, hooked, serrated, pointed or crossed.

❀ Having no teeth to grind foods effectively, birds are limited in how they can process items such as seeds or nuts. Instead, they let their digestive tract do the work, starting by storing and pre-digesting food in the crop, an expanded part of the oesophagus.

❀ The pre-digested food then moves on to the two-part stomach. The first part is a thin-walled glandular structure that provides for more chemical digestion; the second, very muscular and thick-walled portion is the gizzard, where food is mechanically ground. To increase the efficiency of grinding, some birds pick up grit. Unfortunately, they can also ingest lead shot pellets in wetlands where hunting occurs, resulting in lead poisoning, so many areas have banned lead shot and require steel shot instead.

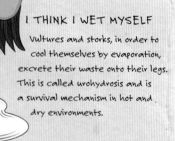

I THINK I WET MYSELF

Vultures and storks, in order to cool themselves by evaporation, excrete their waste onto their legs. This is called urohydrosis and is a survival mechanism in hot and dry environments.

a Grey Plover eating a worm

✈ Aristotle's Hibernating Birds

Aristotle was an early observer of bird migration and his speculations were taken as truths for many years afterwards. For example, he believed that birds hibernated, which was taken as fact until the late nineteenth century. He postulated that the disappearance of many species of birds in the autumn was explained by their passing into a state of torpor while hidden in caves, hollows or marshes. Some early observers even wrote of flocks of swallows in marshes sitting on reeds in such numbers that the reeds bent down into the water where the birds were spending the winter. It was reported that when fishermen drew up their nets, they sometimes had a catch of both fish and hibernating birds.

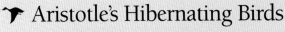

fifteenth-century tile by Luca Della Robbia from the belltower of Santa Maria del Flore in Florence showing Plato and Aristotle (left)

PRODUCTS DANGEROUS TO PET BIRDS

Aerosol sprays

Perfumes

Smoke

Pesticide sprays

Glue

Paints

Self-cleaning ovens

Disinfectants

Cooking gas

Teflon fumes

GREAT BURROWERS

Bee-eaters nest in burrows, which they make by digging with their bills and scraping soil out with their partially fused toes. The burrow may exceed 1 m (1 yd) in length.

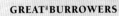

the White-fronted Bee-eater eats bees, wasps and other flying insects

keep items such as glue away from pet birds

Cuckoo Folklore

❀ In Russia, some believe that the cuckoo can predict how many more years a person will live. Upon hearing a cuckoo, a person will reply, 'Cuckoo, how many more years will I live?' The number of cuckoo calls given in reply signifies the number of years left in the person's life.

❀ In certain areas of England, it is considered a bad sign to hear the first cuckoo call before arising from bed.

❀ In Europe, the cuckoo call is considered a harbinger of spring, and the arrival of spring is celebrated in the form of Cuckoo Day in Marsden, England, during the last weekend in April each year. The celebration is based upon a legend with several versions. One of them is that a cuckoo was nesting in a field and in order to keep it around and thus keep perpetual spring, local people added more stones to the field wall, but not enough because the bird flew away. In another version, they tried to trap a cuckoo in a chimney, but it escaped.

❀ In Bangladesh, people believe that the cuckoo is the incarnation of a bereaved husband who lost his wife.

in England, if a milkmaid heard a cuckoo call before she had breakfast, it was believed that she would have a bad day

SUBSONIC BIRDS
Cassowaries, flightless birds of Australia that weigh up to 57 kg (125 lb), produce a booming call so low that humans may not be able to hear it.

KEEPING WOODPECKERS AWAY FROM YOUR HOME

Trouble with woodpeckers drilling your house? Some solutions:

1 Place sheet metal over the area they are drilling.

2 Hang mylar strips, aluminium pie plates or mobiles as scarecrows.

3 Put an artificial owl or snake in the area.

4 Get out and scare the bird whenever you see it.

early twentieth-century illustration of Black-backed Woodpeckers from Birds of New York

ORNITHOMANCY This term refers to a popular form of divination in ancient Rome, purporting to interpret the flight patterns of birds. The result of this divination was known as an auspice, from *avis* (bird) and *spicere* (to observe).

mosaic of Minerva, the Roman goddess of wisdom, symbolized by her owl

MINERVA ROMANA

1880

Four Is the Number

The breeding season is so short in the Arctic and far north that wading birds time their nesting so that hatching of young will occur when the main hatch of insects takes place, thus providing the chicks with abundant food. Most waders lay four eggs in their nests, which may be a shallow depression in the gravel or sand, an area of grass that the birds have stomped down or a cup nest built of plant materials. The eggs are laid with their pointy ends inwards to prevent them from rolling around. Four eggs fit nicely together because they are pointed at one end, which is better for incubation, but three or five eggs would work as well, so why four? Well, in most waders, four eggs laid in less than a week may weigh as much as 25–30 per cent of the female's body weight – equivalent to a woman giving birth to a 18 kg (40 lb) baby. So four is probably the optimum number of eggs.

birdwatchers in Argentina

Birding Statistics

❖ Perhaps as many as 30 per cent of the people of the UK consider themselves birdwatchers. Approximately 550 species of birds have been seen in the UK over the years and any birder (twitcher) who has seen 400 or more can join the UK400 Club.

❖ A recent survey found that 46 million people in the US over the age of 16 consider themselves birdwatchers – nearly one in five individuals. Sixty per cent of these are garden birdwatchers; 40 per cent take trips to see birds.

❖ Of all those calling themselves birdwatchers in the US, 74 per cent were capable of identifying 1–20 species; 14 per cent could identify 21–40 species; and 12 per cent could identify more than 40 species. (Only species in the local area were considered.)

➤ Skimming the Surface

The Black Skimmer is a bird that frequents coastal waters and feeds by skimming the surface of the water with its lower mandible slicing through the water. When it hits a prey item such as a squid or fish, it snaps it up. The lower mandible is thus exposed to considerable wear and tear, but it actually grows faster than the upper mandible. If kept in captivity and not allowed to skim the waters, the lower mandible will grow quite long.

SANDGROUSE SPA

Sandgrouse frequently take dust baths and in the process roll over and lie on their backs with their feet in the air.

SAVING ENERGY

❖ Small birds such as wrens, tits and treecreepers may roost together in segregated or mixed flocks to conserve energy by using each other for insulation. They may save 50 per cent or more of their body heat by doing so on a cold night.

❖ Energy expended per distance travelled is less in flying birds than in walking or running mammals, although it is greater than that of swimming fish.

❖ While in flight some birds travel in an undulating path, alternating flapping their wings and gliding, or just folding their wings against their body and dropping and then flapping again. These flight strategies may reduce the cost of flying by as much as 10 per cent.

small tits roost in flocks to keep warm and conserve energy

Threatened Bird Species' Ranges

Over 70 per cent of bird species considered threatened have home ranges under 50,000 sq km (19,000 sq miles), and about 150 species are restricted to ranges of less than 3100 sq km (8 sq miles).

a Rufous Hummingbird at a garden feeder

Hummingbird Feeders – Do's, Don'ts and Facts

1 Fill the feeder with a boiled sugar:water solution of 1:4 or 1:5 – no artificial sweeteners.

2 A greater concentration of sugar may cause the sugar to crystallize on the birds' bills, leading to bill rot.

3 Keep clean – change the food at least every two days.

4 Red dye will attract the birds faster but they will find the feeder regardless of colour.

5 There is no evidence that red dye in their nectar is harmful.

6 If you do not want to dye the food, tie a red ribbon around the feeder to attract the birds faster.

7 No hummers? They prefer natural nectar, so wait until the flowers die and they will come.

8 Keeping hummingbird feeders up all winter will not stop the birds from migrating.

Birds have to see well in order to fly through trees and branches and spot prey, whether insects or rabbits, from long distances.

✿ The retina of birds, the layer of photosensitive cells at the back of the eye, is comparatively larger than that of humans, with the retina of an eagle containing about fives times the number of cells as a human's. If humans had the ability to see as well as eagles and hawks, we would be able to read a newspaper from 25 m (27 yds) away.

✿ Many birds also have multiple foveas (areas of high concentration of sensory cells) that focus vision. Try this:

1 Hold a finger 60 cm (2 ft) in front of your face. You can see it clearly because you are focusing the image on your one fovea.

2 Now hold your finger 60 cm (2 ft) to the left of your head and move your eyes (but not your head) to see it. It is not in focus because the light from it is not hitting the fovea.

✿ With multiple foveas, most of what birds see is in focus. Some birds, such as hawks, have two foveas, enabling them to see a wide range of in-focus objects. Some seabirds and waders have a ribbon-like fovea across the back of the eye in order to orientate themselves better to the horizon.

the Red-tailed Hawk has superb vision

ASIAN SYMBOL

The Red-crowned Crane, also known as the Japanese Crane, is a symbol of long life, peace, happiness and fidelity to the people of Japan and other Asian countries.

Red-crowned Cranes breed in Siberia and China in summer, then return to East Asia for the winter

CUCKOLDING JACANAS

Jacanas are polyandrous, with a female mating with several males. The males tend to the nest and eggs, and as often as not end up raising some of the chicks from another male. However, since some of the young are also his, it is a reasonable trade-off.

🐦 Migration Is Dangerous

❖ Many thousands of small migratory birds die each year en route to their wintering grounds.

❖ Migratory birds are so reliable that Eleonora's Falcon breeds in the autumn in order to prey upon songbirds that cross the Mediterranean as a source of food for its young.

❖ Only 10–15 per cent of migratory songbirds hatched in one year become breeding adults the following year.

SAPSUCKERS SUCK SAP

Sapsuckers, a kind of woodpecker, drill small holes in tree bark, causing the tree to exude sap to protect itself. Sapsuckers not only lap up the sap with their brush-like tongue, but also eat the insects that come to drink the sap.

BIRD STRIKES

❖ The first recorded fatality due to a bird striking an aircraft occurred in 1912, when an aircraft and gull collided over the coast of California and crashed into the ocean, killing the pilot.

❖ More than 195 people have been killed worldwide as a result of wildlife strikes since 1988.

❖ Bird and other wildlife strikes by aircraft result in $600 million (£300 million) per year in damage to US civil and military airplanes.

Strikes by birds on aircraft can have fatal consequences

Eleonora's Falcon preys upon migrating songbirds

Dodo

DEAD AS A DODO: THE LAST STUFFED DODO WAS DESTROYED IN A FIRE AT OXFORD UNIVERSITY IN ENGLAND IN 1755.

EAGLE HUNTERS

At a time when there was a bounty on eagles, the people of Værøy on Lofoten Islands, Norway, used to catch Golden Eagles with their bare hands. Lying in wait in caves, hunters set bait for the eagles and reached out and caught them when they landed. Eagle hunting caves can still be seen today.

the Golden Eagle is a sacred bird in Native American cultures

SOME BIRDS IN LITERATURE

The Raven, Edgar Allan Poe

Ode to a Nightingale, John Keats

The Eagle, Alfred Lord Tennyson

The Owl and the Pussy-cat, Edward Lear

The Birds, Aristophanes

Nightingale, Hans Christian Andersen

I Know Why the Caged Bird Sings, Maya Angelou

PLUS ONE THIRD

1 In many bird habitats, the length of the breeding season is a third longer than the average length of the breeding season of all the bird species.

2 To calculate the total time during which all the birds in an area breed, add up all the breeding lengths of all the birds in the area, take the average of these and add a third more.

3 In Lapland, for example, the average breeding length for all the species is 0.96 months. It takes 1.32 months (40 days) for all the species in Lapland to breed; 1.32 is about a third longer than 0.96.

Phew, a couple more days and we'd have been stuck in that egg till next year...

Ecological Equivalents

As in many groups of plants and animals, various roles are filled by different species or groups of birds in different places in the world.

✿ In the New World, the hummingbirds are the major nectar feeders; in Africa and Asia, the nectar feeders are the sunbirds.

✿ The meadowlands of North America and the longclaws of Africa both occupy similar grassland niches; although in different families some species have evolved remarkably similar plumages.

✿ No woodpeckers found their way to the Galapagos Islands, but one or more finches did, evolving into 14 species. One of these is the Woodpecker Finch, which not only takes the job of a woodpecker by probing for insects and grubs on tree bark, but does so with the use of a tool. It breaks a twig or cactus spine to an appropriate length and uses it to pry out its prey.

✿ In Alaska, the role of big bird scavenger is partly filled by the Bald Eagle because there are no vultures.

✿ The Green Woodpecker of Europe looks and acts similarly to the Northern Flicker of North America.

♀ Fork-tailed Sunbird feeding on nectar

THUMBING A RIDE

Attached to a bird's thumb is a small group of feathers called an alula or bastard wing. This structure can be moved independently of the wing and serves as a slot to reduce turbulence over the wing, much as slats do on the front of a modern jet plane.

sixth-century BC Attic drinking cup depicting the Trojan War

ALBATROSSES These birds belong to the family Diomedeidae. Diomedes, the Greek hero of the Trojan War, was exiled to an isolated island with his friends, who were all turned into large white birds.

Anna Held, a star in some of Florenz Ziegfeld's Broadway shows, in an extravagant feather hat

THE FEATHER TRADE

❖ In the late 1800s and early 1900s, stylish women wore feather-bedecked hats in the latest designs from Paris and New York. Hat makers from Europe and America traded indiscriminately in feathers and birds to make hats as exotic as possible. Nearly 75 per cent of women in New York wore these types of hats, some of them incorporating whole birds.

❖ At the height of the trade, between 1870 and 1920, untold numbers of white egrets, herons and terns were killed for their feathers (aigrettes). In Paris, more than 10,000 people were employed in the aigrette business.

❖ French military officers adorned their stiff hats with heron feathers. In some places the birds became known as Aigrette Colonels.

❖ In 1885 alone, over 750,000 bird skins were sold. One auction house in London lists more than 1 million heron or egret skins sold between 1897 and 1911.

❖ A single Great White Egret has 40–50 aigrettes, so 150 birds were needed per 1 kg (35 oz) of feathers. In 1902 in London alone, 136 kg (48,000 oz) of feathers were sold, which needed a minimum of 192,000 Great White Egrets.

❖ In 1903, a feather hunter in North America received a price more than twice the weight of the feathers in gold. In India, egret feathers were sold for 15–20 times the price of silver. In Europe, the price was £15 per ounce (28 g) of feathers.

DINOSAUR GLIDERS

Microraptor gui was a feathered flying dinosaur of 125 million years ago. Unlike other flying reptiles, it had two pairs of wings – one on its arms and one on its legs – and a tail with feather fringes, so it flew (or at least glided) like a biplane. Found in China, it is presumed to be an intermediate stage of flight for birds.

a Scaly-throated Honeyguide feeding on a honeycomb

Honeyguides

So called because natives of Africa follow them to bees' nests, honeyguides eat bee larvae and the wax of honeycombs, which they are able to digest with the help of symbiotic bacteria in their gut. This conscious behaviour evolved from the birds leading a carnivore, the honey badger, to bees' nests; the honey badger dismantles the nest and both mammal and bird eat the available food. The birds lead humans to the nests for the same mutual benefit.

AVIAN IQ

A Canadian scientist created an IQ scale of birds, based upon their innovations in feeding – dropping nuts on roadways, using tools and so on – that were reported in scientific journals. The smartest birds? Jays and crows.

FEEDING SUNFLOWER SEED

There are striped and black kinds; black seeds are more bird-friendly than striped because they are easier to open. You can also find whole or bits of sunflower seeds with the hull removed; these are easiest of all for birds to eat.

CHICKEN, ALASKA

In the late 1800s, miners prospected for gold in Alaska. Food was sometimes scarce, but a particular area near the south fork of the 40-Mile River was abundant in Willow Ptarmigan, now the state bird, which looks and perhaps tastes a bit like chicken. In 1902, the settlement became the second town in Alaska to become incorporated. When deciding on a name for the town, Ptarmigan was suggested, but no one could agree on the correct spelling, so the residents settled on Chicken.

black sunflower seeds are easy for birds to open

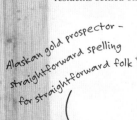

Alaskan gold prospector – straightforward spelling for straightforward folk

The Average Birdwatcher

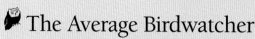

- The most active participants in birding are 55 to 64 years of age.
- The least active participants are between 18 and 24.
- Participation in birding increases proportionately with income and formal education levels.
- The average birder devotes about 10 days a year to birdwatching and lives in the suburbs.

- Keen birders spend most weekends of the year birdwatching, and take a birdwatching holiday, too.

sensible headgear to protect against the sun, the cold – and overhead spillages

waterproof jacket with handwarmer pockets

binoculars for spotting far-off birds

deep pockets for storing maps, field guides and cheese sandwiches

sensible footwear for trekking through marshy fields

HUGIN AND MUNIN

In Norse mythology, Odin used two ravens named Hugin (Thought) and Munin (Memory) to inform him about news around the world. The ravens would travel the world each day and return in the evening to whisper news into the ears of Odin, also known as Raven God.

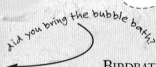

did you bring the bubble bath?

BIRDBATH ESSENTIALS

1 The bigger the birdbath, the better. Smaller birdbaths serve as a source of water for drinking but bigger birdbaths encourage bathing.

2 The slope of the birdbath is important. A birdbath that is too deep will discourage birds; 7.5 cm (3 in) is plenty.

3 The bottom surface of a birdbath should be textured to provide a grip for bird feet.

4 A light colour is recommended for the bottom because it gives the birds a better view of the birdbath and its depth.

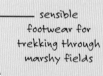

CONDOR CONSUMPTION

In 2005, a young California Condor, removed from its nest because it was sickly, was found to have been fed bottle caps, electrical fittings, washers, gun shells and cartridge casings, pieces of plastic, stones and bits of glass, wire and rubber by its parents.

HOMING OR CARRIER PIGEONS

❖ Homing pigeons were used in ancient Greece to convey the names of Olympic victors to various cities.

❖ Before the telegraph, carrier pigeons were used by stockbrokers to convey information.

❖ Pigeons have been used to report yacht races, with some yachts fitted with lofts.

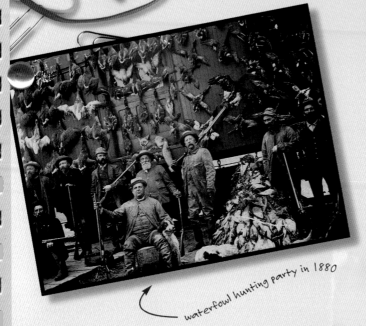

waterfowl hunting party in 1880

PECKING ORDER

The term pecking order derives from studies of how chickens establish dominance in a flock but has come to mean relative social standing in various aspects of society.

Early Conservation

In the late 1800s and early 1900s there began a strong clash between hunting and conservation because birds were being slaughtered in great numbers for food, decoration for hats or clothing, or just for sport. It was pressure to stop the slaughter of birds for the fashion industry (hats), to stop the trapping of small songbirds and to prevent oil spills that fuelled the work of early conservation efforts.

cock-a-doodle-doo
cock-a-doodle-doo
cock-a-doodle-doo

cockerels crow to proclaim their territory

EGG-CELLENT JOB

Howard Helmer, the world's fastest omelette maker, holds the Guinness Book of World Records title for cooking 427 two-egg omelettes in 30 minutes.

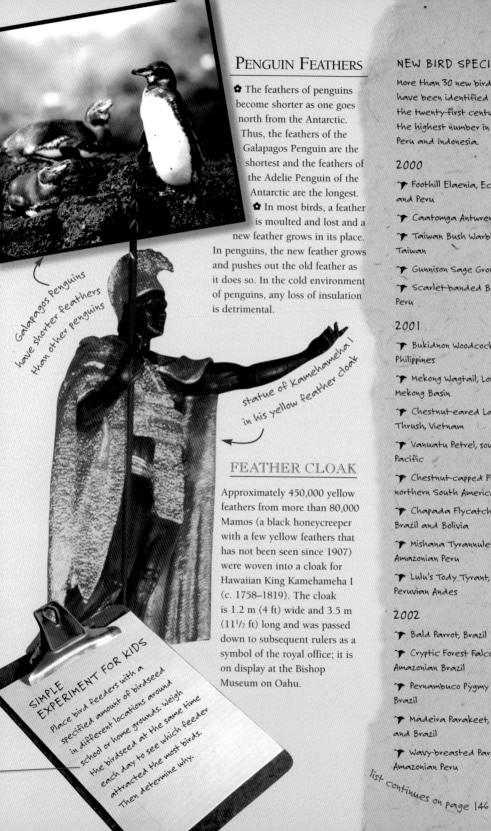

PENGUIN FEATHERS

✿ The feathers of penguins become shorter as one goes north from the Antarctic. Thus, the feathers of the Galapagos Penguin are the shortest and the feathers of the Adelie Penguin of the Antarctic are the longest.

✿ In most birds, a feather is moulted and lost and a new feather grows in its place. In penguins, the new feather grows and pushes out the old feather as it does so. In the cold environment of penguins, any loss of insulation is detrimental.

Galapagos Penguins have shorter feathers than other penguins

statue of Kamehameha I in his yellow feather cloak

FEATHER CLOAK

Approximately 450,000 yellow feathers from more than 80,000 Mamos (a black honeycreeper with a few yellow feathers that has not been seen since 1907) were woven into a cloak for Hawaiian King Kamehameha I (c. 1758–1819). The cloak is 1.2 m (4 ft) wide and 3.5 m (11½ ft) long and was passed down to subsequent rulers as a symbol of the royal office; it is on display at the Bishop Museum on Oahu.

SIMPLE EXPERIMENT FOR KIDS

Place bird feeders with a specified amount of birdseed in different locations around school or home grounds. Weigh the birdseed at the same time each day to see which feeder attracted the most birds. Then determine why.

NEW BIRD SPECIES

More than 30 new bird species have been identified so far in the twenty-first century, with the highest number in Brazil, Peru and Indonesia.

2000

🐦 Foothill Elaenia, Ecuador and Peru

🐦 Caatomga Antwren, Brazil

🐦 Taiwan Bush Warbler, Taiwan

🐦 Gunnison Sage Grouse, US

🐦 Scarlet-banded Barbet, Peru

2001

🐦 Bukidnon Woodcock, Philippines

🐦 Mekong Wagtail, Lower Mekong Basin

🐦 Chestnut-eared Laughing Thrush, Vietnam

🐦 Vanuatu Petrel, southwest Pacific

🐦 Chestnut-capped Piha, northern South America

🐦 Chapada Flycatcher, Brazil and Bolivia

🐦 Mishana Tyrannulet, Amazonian Peru

🐦 Lulu's Tody Tyrant, Peruvian Andes

2002

🐦 Bald Parrot, Brazil

🐦 Cryptic Forest Falcon, Amazonian Brazil

🐦 Pernambuco Pygmy Owl, Brazil

🐦 Madeira Parakeet, Bolivia and Brazil

🐦 Wavy-breasted Parakeet, Amazonian Peru

list continues on page 146

Crested Eagle

BIRDHOUSES FOR DIFFERENT SPECIES

Every species of bird that nests in a cavity requires a different nestbox configuration, so you need to find out the following requirements:

1 Overall size.

2 Specific dimensions of height, width and length.

3 Diameter of the hole.

4 Height of the hole above the floor of the house.

5 Height of the birdhouse from the ground.

6 Habitat that the house should be placed in.

This information can easily be found in a variety of books or on the internet from the British Trust for Ornithology or the Royal Society for the Protection of Birds.

Eyeshades

Like poker players or beach goers, soaring hawks and eagles have an eyeshade. In order to minimize the effect of overhead sunlight, these birds have evolved a cartilaginous ridge over their eyes as a shade. This is what gives them a bit of an ominous appearance.

BIG BIRD, BIG BRAIN? AN OSTRICH'S EYE IS LARGER THAN ITS BRAIN.

choose the right birdhouse for the species you want to nest there

SPEEDY TWO TOES

✿ Ostriches, the only birds with two toes, can run at 70 kph (45 mph) in bursts.
✿ They can maintain 50 kph (30 mph) over a longer period of time.
✿ When running, an ostrich's stride may exceed 7 m (23 ft).

an ostrich can run faster than a zebra

CHICKEN RENAISSANCE
During the Renaissance, chicken broth was said to cure flatulence, arthritis, headaches, indigestion and constipation, while cockerel brains cured cerebral palsy and snakebite. As is the case with many cures of these times, there is no evidence to support them.

new bird species –
list continued from page 144

2003

🐦 Carrizal Seedeater,
Venezuela

🐦 Munchique Wood Wren,
Colombian Andes

🐦 Okarito Brown Kiwi, New
Zealand

2004

🐦 Serendib Scops Owl,
Sri Lanka

🐦 Togian Hawk Owl, Indonesia

🐦 Rubeho Akalat, Tanzania

🐦 Acre Antshrike, Brazil

🐦 Calayan Rail, Philippines

🐦 Mees's Nightjar, Indonesia

list continues on page 147

FEAR OF BIRDS

*This is called ornithophobia.
Movies like Alfred Hitchcock's
The Birds are not the
sufferers' favourite films.*

The Cuckoo and the Cowbird

A few species of birds – nest parasites – have evolved the intriguing habit of letting other birds raise their young.

🌸 The most famous nest parasite is the European Cuckoo, which parasitizes more than 125 species of birds.

🌸 Instead of building a nest, laying eggs, incubating them and raising the young, the female cuckoo finds an active nest of another species, waits until the mother flies off for a short time and in a matter of seconds lays an egg in that nest.

🌸 The returning mother often does not recognize the strange egg because in the cuckoo's evolution, their eggs have come to resemble that of the host in size and colour.

🌸 When the young cuckoo hatches, it attempts, often successfully, to push the other young and eggs over the edge of the nest by scooting backwards against them. The young cuckoo is then raised by the host.

🌸 The host species may be a much smaller bird, such as a Dunnock. The size difference led Pliny, the Roman naturalist, to presume that the young cuckoo ate its host mother when it reached full size.

🌸 The Brown-headed Cowbird of North America is also a nest parasite, laying its eggs in the nests of 144 species of host birds; one female may lay 40 eggs in a season. Although its eggs do not resemble that of the host, the host birds feed the young cowbird more food than their own young.

detail from movie
poster for Hitchcock's
The Birds

AVIAN FLU TRANSMISSION

Although the jury is still out, it appears unlikely that wild birds are the cause of spreading the bird flu virus. Tracking the geographic spread of bird flu, it appears to follow railroad lines and motorways, not migratory pathways, indicating that poultry shipments are the most likely sources of dissemination.

a Yellow Warbler feeding Brown-headed Cowbird nest parasites

new bird species – list continued from page 146

2005

🐦 Sulphur-breasted Parakeet, Amazonian Brazil

🐦 Iquitos Gnatcatcher, Peru

🐦 Stiles's Tapaculo, Colombia

2006

🐦 Camiguin Hanging Parrot, Philippines·

🐦 Bugun Liocichla, India

POETRY AND BIRDS

The expressive language of birds, coupled with the freedom to fly, suggests a relationship with unrestricted speech that has attracted poets such as Emily Dickinson, who wrote in 1924:

To hear the Oriole sing
May be a common thing –
Or only a divine.

early twentieth-century postcard of a medieval falconer

＿ Falconry

✿ Falconry – the sport of hunting prey with falcons – began either in China or the Middle East, although references to falconry go back at least to Aristotle in 384 BC.

✿ Archeological digs in the Middle East suggest that birds may even have been used in falconry as long as 10,000 years ago.

✿ Early stories relate tales of Arabian falconers using birds to attack gazelles.

✿ The Crusaders apparently brought falconry to England; the monarchy then passed laws making falconry the sport of kings and available to nobles alone.

TRIUMPH DISPLAYS

Observed in Canada Geese, Mute Swans and some penguins, a pair of birds will engage in some sort of display or ceremony to celebrate the chasing off of a territorial intruder.

POLISH IT OFF

In modern-day Egypt, scarab carvers feed their artistic creations of limestone, turquoise, serpentine or other material to geese. They pass through the gizzard and emerge with a rough polish.

Egyptian Goose

THE THIRD EYELID

1 Birds have three eyelids: the upper and lower ones close only during sleep, while the third one is used for 'winking'.

2 This nictitating membrane, thin and transparent, extends from the corner of the eye across the eyeball very quickly, cleaning and moisturizing the surface of the eye.

3 The membrane is translucent in most birds, but some diving birds have a clear area in the middle, so it acts like a contact lens while diving.

LOUDEST BIRD

The bellbirds of South America have one of the loudest voices of all birds, capable of being heard 1 km (over half a mile) away.

the nictitating membrane – third eyelid – of a Long-eared Owl

STICK ONE'S HEAD IN THE SAND? OSTRICHES DON'T DO THAT.

Flamingo Nest

The flamingo builds up its large nest like a pedestal, almost 1 m (40 in) wide and with a depression at the top. It lays only one egg. Because of the construction of the nest and the length of the flamingo's legs, a portion of the bird's legs hangs over the outside of the nest.

flamingos with their large pedestal nests

SCHIEFFELIN'S STARLINGS

Eugene Schieffelin, a pharmaceutical manufacturer who had emigrated from Germany to the US, for some reason decided that all the birds mentioned in Shakespeare's plays should be introduced into his new homeland. The only successful introduction of his was the European Starling, introduced into Central Park in New York in 1890 and more later. Today, they are found virtually all over North America except for the extreme northern regions.

a young starling emerging from its nest in a tree

BLUE IMMIGRANT The settler who first introduced the Dunnock to New Zealand was intrigued by its blue eggs.

How Lift Works

One of the reasons birds (and airplanes) can fly is the lift generated by the wings, which are curved convex above and concave below. The air has a longer way to go over the top of the wing than the bottom and thus travels faster. When air speeds up, its pressure becomes lower, so the air moving above the wing has lower pressure than the air moving below it. The higher air pressure below the wing pushes upwards and gives the bird lift. You can demonstrate this with some simple experiments.

1 Hold a piece of paper between thumb and forefinger and place it just below your lower lip. Blow strongly over the top of it. What happens? As the blown air travels faster over the top of the paper, the still air beneath exerts greater pressure and causes the paper to lift.

2 Obtain a hair dryer and a ping pong ball. Turn the hair dryer blower on high speed, turn it so it blows upwards and put the ball in the airstream. It stays there as long as the blower continues. Now slowly tilt the dryer; how far can you tilt the airstream and continue to keep the ball aloft? Instead of gravity causing the ball to fall, the still air below the ball exerts greater pressure than the blown air from the dryer, causing the ball to stay aloft (up to a certain point).

BIRD AND MOTH

Male Green Thorntail hummingbirds guard inga trees when they are in bloom in Colombia and attack any intruders. The female hummingbirds feed on these flowers, but so do White Banded Sphinxlet Moths, similar in appearance to the females. They are so similar, in fact, that the males consider the moths to be potential mates and continue to defend territories against all comers, including Tropical Kingbirds that prey on the moths.

WATCH BIRDS

Trumpeters, South American relatives of cranes, solicit preening by their owners and beg for food from familiar people. They are also valued as 'watch dogs' because they respond to unfamiliar sounds.

WILL THEY FORM A UNION?

Companies that make pills or some kinds of sweets need to remove broken ones from the assembly line. Boring, tedious work for humans, birds have been tried out for the job and found to be much more suited to it, and more accurate as well.

Australia prohibits the export of native wildlife, so all pet cockatiels are bred in captivity, thereby protecting wild populations

Parrots in Danger

According to the Royal Society for the Protection of Birds, the European Union is the world's largest importer of wild-caught parrots. Between 1997 and 2000, the EU imported 469,602 wild birds of 111 species. More parrots are globally threatened with extinction than any other bird family. Trapping for the pet trade and habitat destruction are the causes.

Four Guidelines for Choosing a Field Guide

1 Numerous field guides to birds include anywhere from a few dozen to a few thousand species, depending on the geographical location the guide covers. A field guide to most birds (of either Europe or the US) will have around 600 species in it. If you travel widely, this may be the kind you want. If you only travel in a smaller area, such as the UK or the eastern US, you probably want a less inclusive field guide.

2 A complete field guide is appropriate for experienced birdwatchers, but one with fewer species is better for less experienced people.

3 Go with your own personal preference. Most good field guides are of similar size for ease of use in the field, are arranged in a similar order, and have colour illustrations, species descriptions and range maps.

4 Asking an experienced birdwatcher is probably the best way to choose a book.

buy a good field guide to help you recognize birds, such as the White-bellied Drongo of India

pick the one at the bottom to get the freshest egg

FRESH EGGS: *Place an egg in a container of water; it will sink if fresh. Older eggs float more, because as the moisture in the egg's tissues evaporates, the space this leaves behind fills with air.*

not fresh – a 1,000-year-old egg

CAN YOU IMITATE A BIRD CALL?

Although some people can imitate bird calls that sound authentic to humans, the calls do not sound accurate to birds. Birds' ears are simply much more discriminating than ours. Despite that, efforts to mimic bird songs and calls can be used to attract birds for closer observation.

Trinidad nature centre guide making bird calls to attract wildlife

swallows, such as this Barn Swallow, are just one of the hundreds of bird species mentioned in Shakespeare's plays

LOSING WING FEATHERS

When birds moult their wing feathers, the danger is that they could be subject to aerodynamic imbalances. However, evolution has seen to it that the feathers moult one at a time and symmetrically, so that each wing has the same number of missing feathers at any one time. There are exceptions, though. Waterfowl, for example, undergo an 'eclipse' plumage where all flight feathers are lost simultaneously and the birds are flightless until the feathers grow back.

Birds That Ever Were

❖ Roughly 1,700 species of birds have been identified by fossil remains.

❖ Of this number, about 800 are extant (still living) and 900 extinct.

❖ Over the 150 million or so years in which birds have existed, perhaps 166,000 species have evolved but only about 10,000 now exist – that is, just 6 per cent.

❖ It appears, based upon DNA studies, that the average bird species arises and disappears over a period of about 25,000 years.

Fairy Penguin mannequins modelling knitted sweaters

SHAKESPEARE'S BIRDS

There are at least 600 references to birds in Shakespeare's plays, including the following:

Blackbird	Duck
Bunting	Eagle
Chough	Falcon
Cock	Finch
Cormorant	Fowl
Crow	Goose
Cuckoo	Guinea Hen
Daw	Hedge Sparrow
Divedapper	
Dove	Heron

list continues on page 153

PENGUIN SWEATERS

The Tasmanian Conservation Trust asked volunteers to knit penguin sweaters. Over 1,000 sweaters have been made to fit the small Fairy Penguins that live off the Australian coast to the south. Frequent victims of oil spills, the tiny sweaters prevent the birds from digesting oil while preening and help them to keep warm besides.

Hitchhiking Hummingbirds

Some people say that hummingbirds make their northward spring migration from the Yucatan Peninsula of Mexico to the US mainland on the backs of Canada Geese. No one knows how this myth started but it may be because it is hard to imagine such small birds making a 800 km (500 mile) nonstop flight. Why the hummingbirds should presume to pick geese and no other species is curious, but the fact is they make the journey on their own.

long-tailed hummingbird

the Great Horned Owl is the official bird of Alberta, Canada

LARYNX VS SYRINX

Humans make sounds with their larynx; birds make sounds with an organ called the syrinx that has a specialized set of muscles and membranes over which air flows. Virtually all the air that passes over the syrinx produces sound, while only 2 per cent does so in humans.

Shakespeare's birds – list continued from page 152

Jay	Phoenix
Kestrel	Pigeon
Kingfisher	Popinjay
Kite	Quail
Lapwing	Raven
Lark	Robin
Loon	Rook
Magpie	Seagull
Mallard	Snipe
Martin	Sparrow
Nightingale	Starling
Osprey	Swallow
Ostrich	Swan
Owl	Thrush
Parrot	Turkey
Partridge	Vulture
Peacock	Woodcock
Pelican	Wren
Pheasant	

CANADIAN PROVINCIAL BIRDS

Canada's national bird	Common Loon (Great Northern Diver)
Alberta	Great Horned Owl
British Columbia	Steller's Jay
Manitoba	Great Grey Owl
New Brunswick	Black-capped Chickadee
Newfoundland	Atlantic Puffin
Northwest Territories	Gyrfalcon
Nova Scotia	Osprey
Nunavut	None
Ontario	Common Loon
Prince Edward Island	Blue Jay
Quebec	Snowy Owl
Saskatchewan	Sharp-tailed Grouse
Yukon	Common Raven

✝ Index

❦ Credits

Quarto would like to thank and
acknowledge the following for
supplying images reproduced in
this book:

Key = **a** above, **b** below, **c** centre,
l left, **r** right

8bl Artwork by Olivia
9ar, 26cr, 48al Robin Berry
10b Photo12.com/Cinema Collection
13a Corbis
14al Joe McDonald/Corbis
16al Paul Souders/Corbis
17ar Leif Skoogfors/Corbis
18ac, 144al Penny Cobb
18al Tim Zurowski/Corbis
19al Stuart Westmorland/Corbis
20b Danny Lehman/Corbis
22a Tobias Bernhard/zefa/Corbis
23b Daphne Kinzler/Frank Lane
Picture Agency/Corbis
25b Mary Evans Picture
Library/Alamy
28a Bettmann/Corbis
28bl Fridmar Damm/zefa/Corbis
30 Pat Doyle/Corbis
31bl Ralf Hirschberger/dpa/Corbis
32a Eric and David Hosking/Corbis
34ar Swim Ink 2, LLC/Corbis
35b Kevin Schafer/Corbis
36a Jonathan Blair/Corbis
37a Malcolm Kitto/Papilio/Corbis
38a Roger Tidman/Corbis
39b Joe McDonald/Corbis
40a Adam Woolfitt/Corbis
41a Eric and David Hosking/Corbis
44a Onne van der Wal/Corbis
44b Steven Holt/Vireo
46c Robert Pickett/Corbis
47a Hulton-Deutsch
Collection/Corbis
47b iStockphoto.com/pflorendo
photography
52ar Richard Crossley/Vireo
54a Robert Ridgely/Vireo
56bl David Tipling/Vireo
57br J Alonso A/Vireo
59br Rob Curtis/Vireo
60b Bettmann/Corbis
61a Peter Johnson/Corbis
63a Michael & Patricia Fogden/Corbis
64a Chase Swift/Corbis
66a DK Limited/Corbis
67b Lynda Richardson/Corbis

68bl J Schumacher/Vireo
69 Keren Su/Corbis
71a Academy of Natural Sciences of
Philadelphia/Corbis
72b Paul Souders/Corbis
73a Peter Johnson/Corbis
73b Academy of Natural Sciences of
Philadelphia/Corbis
74a Peter Johnson/Corbis
74br Jonathan Blair/Corbis
75c Tom Stewart/Corbis
77b Universal/The Kobal Collection
80br Hulton-Deutsch
Collection/Corbis
81bl, 107al, 129br Andy Finlay
82 Kevin Schafer/Corbis
83b Chris Hellier/Corbis
84bl DK Limited/Corbis
86b Bettmann/Corbis
87 John James Audubon/Vireo/ANSP
88b Bob Steele/Vireo
89b Creasource/Corbis
92bl Wolfgang Kaehler/Corbis
93ar Peter Johnson/Corbis
93b Charles O'Rear/Corbis
94al William S Clark/Vireo
95 Doug Wechsler/Vireo
96a Eric and David Hosking/Corbis
98a Wayne Bennett/Corbis
99br Joe McDonald/Corbis
100a Lightscapes Photography,
Inc/Corbis
100bl, 106ar Michelle Pickering
102bl, 108ar Harriet, courtesy of
Margaret Robinson
104b Sam Fried/Vireo
111a Staffan Widstrand/Corbis
113a Bettmann/Corbis
116a Scott T Smith/Corbis
117 Tim Laman/Vireo
119a Kennan Ward/Corbis
121b Hulton-Deutsch
Collection/Corbis
122ar Ted Spiegel/Corbis
123b Frans Lanting/Corbis
124b Andy Papdatos/Vireo
125c Ronald Thompson/Frank Lane
Picture Agency/Corbis
126b Rick & Nora Bowers/Vireo
127a Buddy Mays/Corbis
128b Jan Butchofsky-Houser/Corbis
129a Roger Tidman/Corbis
130b Richard Crossley/Vireo
131a Alinari Archives/Corbis
132a Hulton-Deutsch
Collection/Corbis
133a Elio Ciol/Corbis
134a George Armistead/Vireo
135b Adrian Binns/Vireo
136br Winfried
Wisniewski/zefa/Corbis
139a Martin Hale/Vireo

139b Christie's Images/Corbis
140 Bettmann/Corbis
141ar P Davey/Vireo
143c Minnesota Historical
Society/Corbis
144c Robert Holmes/Corbis
145bl Peter Johnson/Corbis
146bl Universal/The Kobal Collection
147al J Schumacher/Vireo
147r Rykoff Collection/Corbis
148ar Roger Tidman/Corbis
148b Bettmann/Corbis
149al Lothar Lenz/zefa/Corbis
150l Martin Harvey/Corbis
151b Catherine Karnow/Corbis
152b Reuters/Corbis

All other images are the copyright
of Quarto Publishing plc. While
every effort has been made to credit
contributors, Quarto would like to
apologize should there have been
any omissions or errors – and would
be pleased to make the appropriate
correction for future editions of
the book.

🐧 Author's acknowledgements

Any book, but especially a fact-based,
illustrated one, requires considerable
time and effort, not only on the part
of the author but all the folks behind
the scenes. Thanks go to Quarto
Publishing and all its fine staff for
initiating the book and doing all the
heavy lifting in its preparation,
especially Michelle Pickering. Special
thanks to Dr James R Karr for his
thorough review and advice. My
wife Carol Burr not only provided
insightful comments on the text,
but also tolerated my many hours on
the computer at home and elsewhere.
I very much appreciate the fine library
facilities at California State University,
Chico, where I spent considerable time
researching information. The website
Ornithology.com allowed Quarto
Publishing to find me and also allowed
me to network with the ornithological
world, opening doors to information
I might otherwise not have found. And
finally to my granddaughter Olivia
who, at her young age, sees the natural
world with a fresh and often surprising
perspective; her excitement and focus
when observing a bug, bird or flower
continually remind me of how
enthralling nature is, especially birds.